KARL MARX
and
FRIEDRICH ENGELS

KARL MARX
and
FRIEDRICH ENGELS

An Introduction to Their Lives and Work
By DAVID RIAZANOV

Translated by Joshua Kunitz
With an Introduction by Dirk J. Struik

Monthly Review Press
New York and London

Originally published by International Publishers Co., Inc.
Copyright © 1927 by International Publishers Co., Inc.

Library of Congress Cataloging in Publication Data

Goldendach, David Borisovich, 1870–1942.
Karl Marx and Friedrich Engels.

Translated from the Russian by Joshua Kunitz.
Reprint of the 1927 ed. published by International Publishers,
New York, which was issued as v. 2 of the Marxist library.
   1. Marx, Karl, 1818–1883.   2.   Engels, Friedrich,
1820–1895.   I. Series: Marxist library, v.2.
HX39.5.G613 1973   335.4'092'2 [B]   73–8055
ISBN 0–85345–297–0

Second Printing

Monthly Review Press
62 West 14th Street, New York, N.Y. 10011
21 Theobalds Road, London WC1X 8SL

Manufactured in the United States of America

CONTENTS

CHAPTER ONE

THE INDUSTRIAL REVOLUTION IN ENGLAND. THE GREAT
FRENCH REVOLUTION AND ITS INFLUENCE UPON GERMANY

CHAPTER TWO

THE EARLY REVOLUTIONARY MOVEMENT IN GERMANY. THE
RHINE PROVINCE. THE YOUTH OF MARX AND ENGELS.
THE EARLY WRITINGS OF ENGELS. MARX AS EDITOR OF
THE *Rheinische Zeitung* . . . .

CHAPTER THREE

THE RELATION BETWEEN SCIENTIFIC SOCIALISM AND PHILOS-
OPHY. MATERIALISM. KANT. FICHTE. HEGEL. FEUER-
BACH. DIALECTIC MATERIALISM. THE HISTORIC MISSION
OF THE PROLETARIAT . . . .

CHAPTER FOUR

THE HISTORY OF THE COMMUNIST LEAGUE. MARX AS AN
ORGANIZER. THE STRUGGLE WITH WEITLING. THE FOR-
MATION OF THE COMMUNIST LEAGUE. *The Communist
Manifesto.* THE CONTROVERSY WITH PROUDHON . .

CHAPTER FIVE

THE GERMAN REVOLUTION OF 1848. MARX AND ENGELS IN
THE RHINE PROVINCE. THE FOUNDING OF THE *Neue
Rheinische Zeitung.* GOTSCHALK AND WILLICH. THE
COLOGNE WORKINGMEN'S UNION. THE POLICIES AND TAC-
TICS OF THE *Neue Rheinische Zeitung.* STEFAN BORN.

FOREWORD

Back in the 1930s when I was planning a course on the economics of socialism at Harvard, I found that there was a dearth of suitable reading material in English on all aspects of the subject, but especially on Marx and Marxism. In combing the relevant shelves of the University library, I came upon a considerable number of titles which were new to me. Many of these of course turned out to be useless, but several contributed importantly to my own education and a few fitted nicely into the need for course reading material. One which qualified under both these headings and which I found to be of absorbing interest was David Riazanov's *Karl Marx and Friedrich Engels* which had been written in the mid-1920s as a series of lectures for Soviet working-class audiences and had recently been translated into English by Joshua Kunitz and published by International Publishers.

I assigned the book in its entirety as an introduction to Marxism as long as I gave the course. The results were good: the students liked it and learned from it not only the main facts about the lives and works of the founders of Marxism, but also, by way of example, something of the Marxist approach to the study and writing of history.

Later on during the 1960s when there was a revival of interest in Marxism among students and others, a growing need was felt for reliable works of introduction and explanation. Given my own past experience, I naturally responded to requests for assistance from students and teachers by recommending, among other works, Riazanov's *Karl Marx and Friedrich Engels*. But by that time the book had long been out of print and could usually be found only in the larger libraries (some of which, as has a way of happening

1

with useful books, had lost their copies in the intervening years). We at Monthly Review Press therefore decided to request permission to reprint the book, and this has now been granted. I hope that students and teachers in the 1970s will share my enthusiasm for a work which exemplifies in an outstanding way the art of popularizing without falsifying or vulgarizing.

In order to enhance the usefulness of the book we enlisted the cooperation of Dirk Struik, asking him to write a scholarly introduction clarifying the place of the book and its author in the mainstream of work on Marx and Engels and Marxism, and add notes where necessary to supplement or correct Riazanov in the light of subsequent Marx scholarship. Professor Struik, in addition to being a distinguished mathematician, is a leading authority in this field. His most recent contribution is the compilation, introduction, and annotation of what may well be the definitive edition of the *Communist Manifesto*.*

Paul M. Sweezy

1973

* *Birth of the Communist Manifesto*, with Full Text of the *Manifesto*, all Prefaces by Marx and Engels, Early Drafts by Engels and Other Supplementary Material. Edited and Annotated and with an Introduction by Dirk J. Struik. New York: International Publishers, 1971, 224 pp. $7.50, $3.25 paper.

INTRODUCTION

D. Riazanov (David Borisovich Goldendach) was born March 10, 1870, in Odessa, Ukraine, then part of Tsarist Russia. As a youth of fifteen, under the influence of P. L. Lavrov, he joined the populist movement of the Narodniki, who went among the people (*narod*—here the peasants) to work for the regeneration of Russia. It brought him five years of prison. He became acquainted with the budding social democratic movement and in 1889 and 1891 visited Russian Marxian circles abroad to acquaint himself with various trends among the political emigrants laying the foundation of the labor movement in Russia (the Russian Social Democratic Party was formed in 1898).

On his return from the second trip, Riazanov was arrested on the frontier, spent fifteen months in prison awaiting trial, and was sentenced to four years of solitary confinement and hard labor. After completing his term of imprisonment he was sent to live in Kishenev, Bessarabia (now Moldavian Soviet Socialist Republic), under police surveillance. Always drawn to the study of social questions, Riazanov got his first opportunity in 1900 when he could go abroad and devote himself to research. His first important work was a critique of the Narodnik movement, *Two Truths* (1901). He had joined the Russian Social Democratic Party and his sympathies were with the group that, being the minority at the Second Party Congress (1903), became known as the Mensheviks. It stressed economic work against political, or approved of political work but opposed the strict disciplinary line laid down by Lenin in *What Is to Be Done?* (1902). After the expulsion of the Mensheviks from the Party in 1912, Riazanov remained in sympathy with them.

In these years Riazanov also began to contribute to *Neue Zeit*, the German Marxist periodical edited by Karl Kautsky. In 1905, immediately after the outbreak of the Revolution, Riazanov returned to Russia and engaged actively in the work of the trade unions of Leningrad (then St. Petersburg). Although arrested again in 1907, he was soon able to leave Russia. He went to Germany and began the research which would make him the leading authority in the documentation of the life and work of Marx and Engels (as the Germans say, *Marx-Forschung*).

To appreciate Riazanov's work we must understand that at the beginning of this century an untold number of documents pertaining to the history of Marxism, even many very important ones, were gathering dust in archives or private collections, or were hidden in newspapers of bygone days. There was little understanding of the value of these documents in leading social-democratic circles, not to speak of academic ones—with few exceptions. This was true for Berlin, where the archives of the Social-Democratic Party (SPD) held most of the literary heritage of Marx and Engels. Riazanov was one of the few who appreciated its meaning for the understanding of the past, present, and future of the socialist movement.

The first task he set himself was the study of Marx's extensive writings on English-Russian relations, especially at the time of the Crimean War (1854–1856), on which he published a monograph in *Neue Zeit* in 1909 (Beiheft 5). In the same year he undertook a study of the First International (1864–1876). Pursuing his research, he moved to London and worked in the British Museum. Here he studied all the publications to which Marx and Engels had contributed between 1852 and 1862, especially the files of the *New York Tribune*, in order to extract their various contributions, often editorials or unsigned articles. These had been partly published by Marx's daughter, Eleanor, and her husband, Edward Aveling, in 1897 in *The Eastern Question*. In 1901

Franz Mehring had published the up-to-then almost unobtainable writings of Marx and Engels for the period 1841–1850) *Aus dem literarischen Nachlass von Karl Marx und Friedrich Engels*, 3 vols.). In 1917, Riazanov, under the auspices of the SPD, published two volumes containing the *Tribune* articles, those in the Chartist *People's Paper*, and several other articles written between 1852 and 1856 (*Gesammelte Schriften von Karl Marx und Friedrich Engels, 1852 bis 1862*, in German translation by Luise Kautsky). Two more volumes were planned, but never appeared. These volumes, together with the correspondence of Marx and Engels published by A. Bebel and E. Bernstein in 1913 (*Briefwechsel*, 4 vols.), form the main contributions to the *Marx-Forschung* before the Russian Revolution.

The publication of Riazanov's research on the First International was planned for 1914. The book was already in type, but the war intervened and it remained unpublished. Part of Riazanov's material was later published in the *Marx-Engels Archiv*, I (1926). Riazanov more than once came in conflict with the opinions of Mehring on the role of such figures as Bakunin and Lassalle. Sometimes he also differed from Marx and Engels, as in their accounts of the origin of the Communist League—written from memory many years after the events. The present book contains some of this criticism.

After the February revolution of 1917 Riazanov returned to Russia, where he was active in the rapidly growing Workers Councils (the Soviets). In August 1917 he joined the Bolshevik Party (in March 1918 renamed the Communist Party), but did not always see eye to eye with Lenin.

The October revolution brought the Bolsheviks to power and gave Riazanov the opportunity to place his knowledge and energy at the service of the new state. In 1918 he began to organize archives, in 1919 he helped to found the Socialist (later Communist) Academy, and started to build up a "cabinet for the history of Marxism" inside the Academy. In 1920, when the now famous Marx-Engels (since 1931, Marx-Engels-Lenin) Institute was founded under the auspices of the Communist Party, Riazanov became its director. The Institute, although first under the Socialist Academy, was from 1922 directly under the Soviet government. Lenin, despite his many other responsibilities, took a direct interest. Together with a number of associates, Riazanov could now devote all his energy to the collection and study of material dealing with the origins and development of the socialist movement throughout the world.

Top priority was given to the preparation of the collected works of Marx and Engels, officially sanctioned in January 1924 at the Thirteenth Congress of the Russian Communist Party and confirmed later that year at the Fifth Congress of the Communist International. This was easier said than done. The Institute had to start nearly from scratch since it began with little more than a few hundred old books and exactly eight original documents. It suffered from a lack of reliable early editions published while Marx and Engels were still alive, and moreover, the later editions by Bernstein and Kautsky were incomplete and not always reliable. But by 1920 Soviet emissaries were busy in London purchasing rare copies of Marxist classics, and Lenin, in a letter of February 1921, asked Riazanov, "Could we not buy the letters of Marx and Engels from Scheidemann and Co. (they are such mercenary rabble),* or purchase photo-copies?" Riazanov set to work.

In 1921 he was in Berlin. Work was not easy because of the anti-Communism of "Scheidemann and Co.," yet after two years of negotiations he was able to send 7,000 photostatic copies back to Moscow. In 1924 he bought for 4,200 marks (about $1000) all rights to the writings of Marx and Engels held in the archives of the German Social Democratic

---

* Philip Scheidemann (1865-1939) was a leading German Social Democrat.

Party. Some years later the SPD tried to back out of the agreement, but by this time it was too late; the Institute had acquired most of what it wanted.

Riazanov also tapped other sources: in Trier (Treves), where Marx had gone to school, in Jena, where he had received his doctoral degree, in the Ruhr region among the descendants of Engels' father. He had correspondents in Britain, France, and the United States tracking down documents in private collections and at auctions. The Institute acquired entire libraries with sociological material on Russia, Germany, Britain, and France. By 1930 it possessed hundreds of original documents, 55,000 pages of photostats, 32,000 pamphlets, and a library of 450,000 books and bound periodicals. Apart from the administrative offices, the archive, and the library, it had working rooms, a museum, and a publishing department.

The main publishing effort was directed toward the achievement of as complete an edition of the works of Marx and Engels, both in Russian and in the original languages, as was possible. The Russian edition was eventually completed in twenty-eight volumes (1931–1951). Of the other edition, five volumes had been published in Germany when Hitler came to power, and two further volumes were published in Leningrad before the enterprise was discontinued in 1935. The seven volumes form the celebrated *Marx-Engels Gesamtausgabe*, affectionately known as MEGA. Although it went only as far as 1848, it made available for the first time such works as the *German Ideology*, the *Economic and Philosophic Manuscripts of 1844*, and the complete set of articles in the *Neue Rheinische Zeitung* up to December 1848. Riazanov also published the *Dialectics of Nature*, but this was in the *Marx-Engels Archiv*, a periodical issued by the Institute, and only two volumes appeared (1926, 1927; later continued in Russian).

With due appreciation for this work, we have to add that not all of it was very carefully done. This was in part due to the difficulty in deciphering Marx's handwriting,* and, sometimes, Engels'. As a result, the *Dialectics of Nature* had to be republished in 1935.

In addition, the Institute published many works of standard Marxian authors such as Plekhanov, Kautsky, Lafargue, and Wilhelm Liebknecht. Among Riazanov's own writings of this period we should mention the two-volume *Essays on the History of Marxism* (1923, 1928, in Russian) and an edition of the *Communist Manifesto* with ample commentary. The latter exists in English translation (1930, reprinted 1958).

We have a description of Riazanov in this period by a comrade who knew him: "The impression he left was one of immense, almost volcanic energy—his powerful build added to this impression—and tirelessness in collecting every scrap about, or pertaining to, Marx and Engels. His speeches at Party congresses, marked by great wit, often carried him in sheer enthusiasm beyond the bounds of logic. He did not hesitate to cross swords with anyone, not even with Lenin. He was treated for this reason with rather an amused respect, as a kind of caged lion, but one whose bark or growl usually had in it a grain or two of truth worth listening to, if you didn't confuse it with the overlay of sarcastic exaggeration.

"I thought his appointment to the Institute was a kind of diversion of his energies into safe but extraordinarily useful channels—and for years I think that was justified."

In March 1930, on his sixtieth birthday, Riazanov's research into socialist history was recognized in a Festschrift entitled *Na boevom postu* (On the Battle Line).

Riazanov's last years were an anticlimax. His Menshevik sympathies had long been tolerated in view of his enormous

---

* Deciphering Marx's handwriting is a science in itself. There now exists, for the work on the planned new edition of the work of Marx and Engels in one hundred volumes, a guide to his handwriting known as the *Müller Primer*, written by retired Detective Officer Kurt Müller of the GDR, who learned graphology in a Nazi prison.

services to the Institute. But the political climate of the early 1930s was not healthy for a man of his type. He seems to have gone just once too far. In 1931, at the trial of the Mensheviks, who had built a secret organization, he was accused of giving it some support within the Institute. This was believed and led to his expulsion from the party. He had to spend some time in prison, and then, in the same year, was sent to Saratov as a librarian. His place as director of the Institute was taken by V. V. Adoratski (1878–1945), who held this position until 1939 and assiduously continued the collecting, editing, and publishing work of his predecessor. Riazanov, greatly at a loss in a provincial town, petitioned for a change and, with the permission of Kirov, was allowed to continue research in Leningrad. However, after Kirov's assassination in 1935 he had to return to Saratov. He died in 1938.

The present volume is the result of a series of popular lectures given by Riazanov in the early years of the Socialist Academy. He gave not only an account of the development of the genius of Marx and Engels, but also a description of the time and the social conditions under which they grew from youth through manhood to advancing age. At the time the lectures were published in book form there existed only one authoritative biography of Marx, by Franz Mehring (1918, English translation 1935), and very little had as yet been written about the life of Engels (the first volume of Gustav Mayer's biography appeared in 1920, but covered only the period until 1851). Riazanov's book lacks the broad design of the Mehring book, but makes use of Riazanov's own research, gives his version of certain periods in the life of Marx and Engels, and leads up to the time of Engels' death in 1895.

The English translation is by Joshua Kunitz, to whom many of the original quotations that appeared in the book were supplied by the Marx-Engels Institute. It was published in New York in 1927 by International Publishers, with a

Preface by its director, Alexander Trachtenberg, which served as basis for the present Introduction.

The present edition is a reproduction of the 1927 translation. This Introduction has been added, as well as a set of notes commenting on places in the text that need some revision or amendment.

Dirk J. Struik

1973

KARL MARX
and
FRIEDRICH ENGELS

CHAPTER I

IN Karl Marx and Friedrich Engels we have two individuals who have greatly influenced human thought. The personality of Engels recedes somewhat into the background as compared to Marx. We shall subsequently see their interrelation. As regards Marx one is not likely to find in the history of the nineteenth century a man who, by his activity and his scientific attainments, had as much to do as he, with determining the thought and actions of a succession of generations in a great number of countries. Marx has been dead more than forty years. Yet he is still alive. His thought continues to influence, and to give direction to, the intellectual development of the most remote countries, countries which never heard of Marx when he was alive.

We shall attempt to discern the conditions and the surroundings in which Marx and Engels grew and developed. Every one is a product of a definite social milieu. Every genius creating something new, does it on the basis of what has been accomplished before him. He does not sprout forth from a vacuum. Furthermore, to really determine the magnitude of a genius, one must first ascertain the antedating achievements, the degree of the intellectual development of society, the social forms into which this genius was born and from which he drew his psychological and physical sus-

13

tenance. And so, to understand Marx—and this is a practical application of Marx's own method—we shall first proceed to study the historical background of his period and its influence upon him.

Karl Marx was born on the 5th of May, 1818, in the city of Treves, in Rhenish Prussia; Engels, on the 28th of November, 1820, in the city of Barmen of the same province. It is significant that both were born in Germany, in the Rhine province, and at about the same time. During their impressionable and formative years of adolescence, both Marx and Engels came under the influence of the stirring events of the early thirties of the nineteenth century. The years 1830 and 1831 were revolutionary years; in 1830 the July Revolution occurred in France. It swept all over Europe from West to East. It even reached Russia and brought about the Polish Insurrection of 1831.

But the July Revolution in itself was only a culmination of another more momentous revolutionary upheaval, the consequences of which one must know to understand the historical setting in which Marx and Engels were brought up. The history of the nineteenth century, particularly that third of it which had passed before Marx and Engels had grown into socially conscious youths, was characterised by two basic facts: The Industrial Revolution in England, and the Great Revolution in France. The Industrial Revolution in England began approximately in 1760 and extended over a prolonged period. Having reached its zenith towards the end of the eighteenth century, it came to an end at about 1830. The ·term "Industrial Revolution" belongs to Engels.* It refers to that transition period, when England, at about the second half of the eighteenth century, was becoming a capitalist country. There already existed a working class, proletarians—that is, a class of people possessing no property, no means of production, and compelled therefore to sell themselves as a commodity, as human labour

* All notes in the text indicated by an asterisk or dagger will be found at the end of the book.

power, in order to gain the means of subsistence. However, in the middle of the eighteenth century, English capitalism was characterised in its methods of production by the handicraft system. It was not the old craft production where each petty enterprise had its master, its two or three journeymen, and a few apprentices. This traditional handicraft was being crowded out by capitalist methods of production. About the second half of the eighteenth century, capitalist production in England had already evolved into the manufacturing stage. The distinguishing feature of this manufacturing stage was an industrial method which did not go beyond the boundaries of handicraft production, in spite of the exploitation of the workers by the capitalists and the considerable size of the workrooms. From the point of view of technique and labour organisation it differed from the old handicraft methods in a few respects. The capitalist brought together from a hundred to three hundred craftsmen in one large building, as against the five or six people in the small workroom heretofore. No matter what craft, given a number of workers, there soon appeared a high degree of division of labour with all its consequences. There was then a capitalist enterprise, without machines, without automatic mechanisms, but in which division of labour and the breaking up of the very method of production into a variety of partial operations had gone a long way forward. Thus it was just in the middle of the eighteenth century that the manufacturing stage reached it apogee.

Only since the second half of the eighteenth century, approximately since the sixties, have the technical bases of production themselves begun to change. Instead of the old implements, machines were introduced. This invention of machinery was started in that branch of industry which was the most important in England, in the domain of textiles. A series of inventions, one after another, radically changed the technique of the weaving and spinning trades. We shall not enumerate all the inventions. Suffice it to say that in about the eighties, both spinning and weaving looms were invented. In 1785, Watt's perfected steam-engine was invented. It enabled the manufactories to be established in cities instead of being restricted to the banks of rivers to obtain water power. This in its turn created favourable conditions for the centralisation and concentration of production. After the introduction of the steam-engine, attempts to utilise steam as motive power were being made in many branches of industry.. But progress was not as rapid as is sometimes claimed in books. The period from 1760 to 1830 is designated as the period of the great Industrial Revolution.

Imagine a country where for a period of seventy years new inventions were incessantly introduced, where production was becoming ever more concentrated, where a continuous process of expropriation, ruin and annihilation of petty handicraft production, and the destruction of small weaving and spinning workshops were inexorably going on. Instead of craftsmen there came an ever-increasing host of proletarians. Thus in place of the old class of workers, which had begun to develop in the sixteenth and seventeenth centuries, and which in the first half of the eighteenth century still constituted a negligible portion of the population of England, there appeared towards the end of the eighteenth and the beginning of the nineteenth centuries, a class of workers which comprised a considerable portion of the population, and which determined and left a definite imprint on all contemporary social relations. Together with this Industrial Revolution there occurred a certain concentration in the ranks of the working class itself. This fundamental change in economic relations, this uprooting of the old weavers and spinners from their habitual modes of life, was superseded by conditions which forcefully brought to the mind of the worker the painful difference between yesterday and to-day.

Yesterday all was well; yesterday there were inherited firmly established relations between the employers and the workers. Now everything was changed and the employers relentlessly threw out of employment tens and hundreds of these workers. In response to this basic change in the conditions of their very existence the workers reacted energetically. Endeavouring to get rid of these new conditions they rebelled. It is obvious that their unmitigated hatred, their burning indignation should at first have been directed against the visible symbol of this new and powerful revolution, the machine, which to them personified all the misfortune, all the evils of the new system. No wonder that at the beginning of the nineteenth century a series of revolts of the workers directed against the machine and the new technical methods of production took place. These revolts attained formidable proportions in England in 1815. (The weaving loom was finally perfected in 1813). About that time the movement spread to all industrial centres. From a purely elemental force, it was soon transformed into an organised resistance with appropriate slogans and efficient leaders. This movement directed against the introduction of machinery is known in history as the movement of the Luddites.

According to one version this name was derived from the name of a worker; according to another, it is connected with a mythical general, Lud, whose name the workers used in signing their proclamations.

The ruling classes, the dominant oligarchy, directed the most cruel repressions against the Luddites. For the destruction of a machine as well as for an attempt to injure a machine, a death penalty was imposed. Many a worker was sent to the gallows.

There was a need for a higher degree of development of this workers' movement and for more adequate revolutionary propaganda. The workers had to be informed that the fault was not with the machines, but with the conditions under which these machines were being used. A movement which was aiming to mould the workers into a class-conscious revolutionary mass, able to cope with definite social and political problems was just then beginning to show vigorous signs of life in England. Leaving out details, we must note, however, that this movement of 1815-1817 had its beginnings at the end of the eighteenth century. To understand, however, the significance of it, we must turn to France; for without a thorough grasp of the influence of the French Revolution, it will be difficult to understand the beginnings of the English labour movement.

The French Revolution began in 1789, and reached its climax in 1793. From 1794, it began to diminish in force. This brought about, within a few years, the establishment of Napoleon's military dictatorship. In 1799, Napoleon accomplished his coup d'état. After having been a Consul for five years, he proclaimed himself Emperor and ruled over France up to 1815.

To the end of the eighteenth century, France was a country ruled by an absolute monarch, not unlike that of Tsarist Russia. But the power was actually in the hands of the nobility and the clergy, who, for monetary compensation of one kind or another, sold a part of their influence to the growing financial-commercial bourgeoisie. Under the influence of a strong revolutionary movement among the masses of the people—the petty producers, the peasants, the small and medium tradesmen who had no privileges—the French monarch was compelled to grant some concessions. He convoked the so-called Estates General. In the struggle between two distinct social groups—the city poor and the privileged classes—power fell into the hands of the revolutionary petty bourgeoisie and the Paris workers. This was on August 10, 1792. This domination expressed itself in the rule of the Jacobins headed by Robespierre and Marat, and one may also add the name of Danton. For two years France was in the hands of the insurgent people. In the vanguard stood revolutionary Paris. The Jacobins, as representatives of the petty bourgeoisie, pressed the demands of their class to their logical conclusions. The leaders, Marat, Robespierre and Danton, were petty-bourgeois democrats who had taken upon themselves the solution of the problem which confronted the entire bourgeoisie, that is, the purging of France of all the remnants of the feudal régime, the creating of free political conditions under which private property would continue unhampered and under which small proprietors would not be hindered from receiving reasonable incomes through honest exploitation of others. In this strife for the creation of new political conditions and the struggle against feudalism, in this conflict with the aristocracy and with a united Eastern Europe which was attacking France, the Jacobins—Robespierre and Marat—performed the part of revolutionary leaders. In their fight against all of Europe they had to resort to revolutionary propaganda. To hurl the strength of the populace, the mass, against the strength of the feudal lords and the kings, they brought into play the slogan: "War to the palace, peace to the cottage." On their banners they inscribed the slogan: "Liberty, Equality, Fraternity."

These first conquests of the French Revolution were reflected in the Rhine province. There, too, Jacobin societies were formed. Many Germans went as volunteers into the French army. In Paris some of them took part in all the revolutionary associations. During all this time the Rhine province was greatly influenced by the French Revolution, and at the beginning of the nineteenth century, the younger generation was still brought up under the potent influence of the heroic traditions of the Revolution. Even Napoleon, who was a usurper, was obliged, in his war against the old monarchical and feudal Europe, to lean upon the basic

victories of the French Revolution, for the very reason
that he was a usurper, the foe of the feudal régime. He
commenced his military career in the revolutionary army.
The vast mass of the French soldiers, ragged and poorly
armed, fought the superior Prussian forces, and defeated
them. They won by their enthusiasm, their numbers. They
won because before shooting bullets they hurled manifestoes,
thus demoralising and disintegrating the enemy's armies.
Nor did Napoleon in his campaigns shun revolutionary
propaganda. He knew quite well that cannon was a splendid
means, but he never, to the last days of his life, disdained
the weapon of revolutionary propaganda—the weapon that
disintegrates so efficiently the armies of the adversary.[*]

The influence of the French Revolution spread further
East; it even reached St. Petersburg. At the news of the
fall of the Bastille, people embraced and kissed one another
even there.

There was already in Russia a small group of people who
reacted quite intelligently to the events of the French Revolution, the outstanding figure being Radishchev.[†] This influence was more or less felt in all European countries; even
in that very England which stood at the head of nearly all
the coalition armies directed against France. It was strongly
felt not only by the petty-bourgeois elements but also by
the then numerous labouring population which came into
being as a result of the Industrial Revolution. In the years
1791 and 1792 the Corresponding Society, the first English
revolutionary labour organisation, made its appearance.
It assumed such an innocuous name merely to circumvent
the English laws which prohibited any society from entering
into organisational connections with societies in other towns.

By the end of the eighteenth century, England had a constitutional government. She already had known two revolutions—one in the middle, the other at the end, of the sev-

enteenth century.[1] She was regarded as the freest country in the world. Although clubs and societies were allowed, not one of them was permitted to unite with the other. To overcome this interdict those societies, which were made up of workers, hit upon the following method: They formed Corresponding Societies wherever it was possible—associations which kept up a constant correspondence among themselves. At the head of the London society was the shoemaker, Thomas Hardy (1752-1832). He was a Scotchman of French extraction. Hardy was indeed what his name implied. As organiser of this society he attracted a multitude of workers, and arranged gatherings and meetings. Owing to the corrosive effect of the Industrial Revolution on the old manufactory production, the great majority of those who joined the societies were artisans—shoemakers and tailors. The tailor, Francis Place, should also be mentioned in this connection, for he, too, was a part of the subsequent history of the labour movement in England. One could mention a number of others, the majority of whom were handicraftsmen. But the name of Thomas Holcroft (1745-1809), shoemaker, poet, publicist and orator, who played an important rôle at the end of the eighteenth century, must be given.

In 1792, when France was declared a republic, this Corresponding Society availed itself of the aid of the French ambassador in London and secretly dispatched an address, in which it expressed its sympathy with the revolutionary convention. This address, one of the first manifestations of international solidarity and sympathy, made a profound impression upon the convention. It was a message from the masses of England where the ruling classes had nothing but hatred for France. The convention responded with a special resolution, and these relations between the workers' Corresponding Societies and the French Jacobins were a pretext

[1] 1642 and 1688.

for the English oligarchy to launch persecutions against these societies. A series of prosecutions were instituted against Hardy and others.

The fear of losing its domination impelled the English oligarchy to resort to drastic measures against the rising labour movement. Associations and societies which heretofore had been a thoroughly legal method of organisation for the well-to-do bourgeois elements, and which the handicraftsmen could not by law be prevented from forming, were, in 1800, completely prohibited. The various workers' societies which had been keeping in touch with each other were particularly persecuted. In 1799 the law specifically forbade all organisations of workers in England. From 1799 to 1824 the English working class was altogether deprived of the right of free assembly and association.

To return to 1815. The Luddite movement, whose sole purpose was the destruction of the machine, was succeeded by a more conscious struggle. The new revolutionary organisations were motivated by the determination to change the political conditions under which the workers were forced to exist. Their first demands included freedom of assembly, freedom of association, and freedom of the press. The year 1817 was ushered in with a stubborn conflict which culminated in the infamous "Manchester Massacre" of 1819. The massacre took place on St. Peter's Field, and the English workers christened it the Battle of Peterloo. Enormous masses of cavalry were moved against the workers, and the skirmish ended in the death of several scores of people. Furthermore, new repressive measures, the so-called Six Acts ("Gag Laws"), were directed against the workers. As a result of these persecutions, revolutionary strife became more intense. In 1824, with the participation of Francis Place (1771-1854), who had left his revolutionary comrades and succeeded in becoming a prosperous manufacturer, but who maintained his relations with the radicals in the House of

Commons, the English workers won the famous Coalition Laws (1824-25) as a concession to the revolutionary movement. The movement in favour of creating organisations and unions through which the workers might defend themselves against the oppression of the employers, and obtain better conditions for themselves, higher wages, etc., became lawful. This marks the beginning of the English trade union movement. It also gave birth to political societies which began the struggle for universal suffrage.

Meanwhile, in France, in 1815, Napoleon had suffered a crushing defeat, and the Bourbon monarchy of Louis XVIII was established. The era of Restoration, beginning at that time, lasted approximately fifteen years. Having attained the throne through the aid of foreign intervention (Alexander I of Russia), Louis made a number of concessions to the landlords who had suffered by the Revolution. The land could not be restored to them, it remained with the peasants, but they were consoled by a compensation of a billion francs. The royal power used all its strength in an endeavour to arrest the development of new social and political relations. It tried to rescind as many of the concessions to the bourgeoisie as it was forced to make. Owing to this conflict between the liberals and the conservatives, the Bourbon dynasty was forced to face a new revolution which broke out in July, 1830.

England which had towards the end of the eighteenth century reacted to the French Revolution by stimulating the labour movement, experienced a new upheaval as a result of the July Revolution in France. There began an energetic movement for a wider suffrage. According to the English laws, that right had been enjoyed by an insignificant portion of the population, chiefly the big landowners, who not infrequently had in their dominions depopulated boroughs with only two or three electors ("Rotten Boroughs"), and who, nevertheless, sent representatives to Parliament.

The dominant parties, actually two factions of the landed aristocracy, the Tories and the Whigs, were compelled to submit. The more liberal Whig Party, which felt the need for compromise and electoral reforms, finally won over the conservative Tories. The industrial bourgeoisie were granted the right to vote, but the workers were left in the lurch.* As answer to this treachery of the liberal bourgeoisie (the ex-member of the Corresponding Society, Place, was a party to this treachery), there was formed in 1836, after a number of unsuccessful attempts, the London Working-men's Association. This Society had a number of capable leaders. The most prominent among them were William Lovett (1800-1877) and Henry Hetherington (1792-1849). In 1837, Lovett and his comrades formulated the fundamental political demands of the working class. They aspired to organise the workers into a separate political party. They had in mind, however, not a definite working-class party which would press its special programme as against the programme of all the other parties, but one that would exercise as much influence, and play as great a part in the political life of the country, as the other parties. In this bourgeois political milieu they wanted to be the party of the working class. They had no definite aims, they did not propose any special economic programme directed against the entire bourgeois society. One may best understand this, if one recalls that in Australia and New Zealand there are such labour parties, which do not aim at any fundamental changes in social conditions. They are sometimes in close coalition with the bourgeois parties in order to insure for labour a certain share of influence in the government.

The Charter, in which Lovett and his associates formulated the demands of the workers, gave the name to this Chartist movement. The Chartists advanced six demands: Universal suffrage, vote by secret ballot, parliaments elected annually, payment of members of parliament, abolition of property qualifications for members of parliament, and equalisation of electoral districts.

This movement began in 1837, when Marx was nineteen, and Engels seventeen years old. It reached its height when Marx and Engels were mature men.

The Revolution of 1830 in France removed the Bourbons, but instead of establishing a republic which was the aim of the revolutionary organisations of that period, it resulted in a constitutional monarchy, headed by the representatives of the Orléans dynasty. At the time of the Revolution of 1789 and later, during the Restoration period, this dynasty stood in opposition to their Bourbon relatives. Louis Philippe was the typical representative of the bourgeoisie. The chief occupation of this French monarch was the saving and hoarding of money, which delighted the hearts of the shopkeepers of Paris.

The July monarchy gave freedom to the industrial, commercial, and financial bourgeoisie. It facilitated and accelerated the process of enrichment of this bourgeoisie, and directed its onslaughts against the working class which had manifested a tendency toward organisation.

In the early thirties, the revolutionary societies were composed chiefly of students and intellectuals. The workers in these organisations were few and far between. Nevertheless a workers' revolt as a protest against the treachery of the bourgeoisie broke out in 1831, in Lyons, the centre of the silk industry. For a few days the city was in the hands of the workers. They did not put forward any political demands. Their banner carried the slogan: "Live by work, or die in battle." They were defeated in the end, and the usual consequences of such defeats followed. The revolt was repeated in Lyons in 1834. Its results were even more important than those of the July Revolution. The latter stimulated chiefly the so-called democratic, petty-bourgeois elements, while the Lyons revolts exhibited, for

the first time, the significance of the labour element, which
had raised, though so far in only one city, the banner of
revolt against the entire bourgeoisie, and had pushed the
problems of the working class to the fore. The principles
enunciated by the Lyons proletariat were as yet not directed
against the foundations of the bourgeois system, but they
were demands flung against the capitalists and against exploitation.

Thus toward the middle of the thirties in both France
and England there stepped forth into the arena a new revolutionary class—the proletariat. In England, attempts were
being made to organise this proletariat. In France, too,
subsequent to the Lyons revolt, the proletariat for the first
time tried to form revolutionary organisations. The most
striking representative of this movement was Auguste Blanqui (1805-1881), one of the greatest French revolutionists.
He had taken part in the July Revolution, and, impressed
by the Lyons revolts which had indicated that the most
revolutionary element in France were the workers, Blanqui
and his friends proceeded to organise revolutionary societies
among the workers of Paris. Elements of other nationalities were drawn in—German, Belgians, Swiss, etc. As a
result of this revolutionary activity, Blanqui and his comrades made a daring attempt to provoke a revolt. Their
aim was to seize political power and to enforce a number of
measures favouring the working class. This revolt in Paris
(May, 1839), terminated in defeat. Blanqui was condemned
to life imprisonment. The Germans who took part in these
disturbances also felt the dire consequences of defeat. Karl
Schapper (1812-1870),* who will be mentioned again, and
his comrades were forced to flee from France a few months
later. They made their way to London and continued their
work there by organising, in 1840, the Workers' Educational
Society.

By this time Marx had reached his twenty-second and Engels his twentieth year.* The highest point in the development of a proletarian revolutionary movement is contemporaneous with their attaining manhood.

CHAPTER II

WE shall now pass on to the history of Germany after 1815. The Napoleonic wars came to an end. These wars were conducted not only by England, which was the soul of the coalition, but also by Russia, Germany and Austria. Russia took such an important part that Tsar Alexander I, "the Blessed," played the chief rôle at the infamous Vienna Congress (1814-15), where the destinies of many nations were determined. The course that events had taken, following the peace concluded at Vienna, was not a whit better than the chaos which had followed the Versailles arrangements at the end of the last imperialist war. The territorial conquests of the revolutionary period were wrenched from France. England grabbed all the French colonies, and Germany, which expected unification as a result of the War of Liberation, was split definitely into two parts. Germany in the north and Austria in the south.*

Shortly after 1815, a movement was started among the intellectuals and students of Germany, the cardinal purpose of which was the establishment of a United Germany. The arch enemy was Russia, which immediately after the Vienna Congress, had concluded the Holy Alliance with Prussia and Austria against all revolutionary movements. Alexander I and the Austrian Emperor were regarded as its founders. In reality it was not the Austrian Emperor, but the main engineer of Austrian politics, Metternich, who was

28

the brains of the Alliance.   But it was Russia that was considered the mainstay of reactionary tendencies ; and when the liberal movement of intellectuals and students started with the avowed purpose of advancing culture and enlightenment among the German people as a preparation for unification, the whole-hearted hatred of this group was reserved for Russia, the mighty prop of conservatism and reaction. In 1819 a student, Karl Sand, killed the German writer August Kotzebue, who was suspected, not without reason, of being a Russian spy.   This terrorist act created a stir in Russia, too, where Karl Sand was looked up to as an ideal by many of the future Decembrists, and it served as a pretext for Metternich and the German government to swoop down upon the German intelligentsia.   The student societies, however, proved insuppressible ; they grew even more aggressive, and the revolutionary organisations in the early twenties sprung up from their midst.

We have mentioned the Russian Decembrist movement which led to an attempt at armed insurrection, and which was frustrated on December 14, 1825.   We must add that this was not an isolated, exclusively Russian phenomenon. This movement was developing under the influence of the revolutionary perturbations among the intelligentsia of Poland, Austria, France, and even Spain.   This movement of the intelligentsia had its counterpart in literature, its chief representative being Ludwig Börne, a Jew, a famous German publicist during the period of 1818-1830 and the first political writer in Germany.   He had a profound influence upon the evolution of German political thought. He was a thoroughgoing political democrat, who took little interest in social questions, believing that everything could be set right by granting the people political freedom.

This went on until 1830.   In that year the July Revolution shook France, and its reverberations set Germany aquiver.   Rebellions and uprisings occurred in several localities, but were brought to an end by some constitutional concessions. The government made short shrift of this movement which was not very deeply rooted in the masses.

A second wave of agitation rolled over Germany, when the unsuccessful Polish rebellion of 1831, which also was a direct consequence of the July Revolution, caused a great number of Polish revolutionists, fleeing from persecution, to seek refuge in Germany. Hence a further strengthening of the old tendency among the German intelligentsia—a hatred for Russia and sympathy for Poland, then under Russian domination.

After 1831, as a result of the two events mentioned above, and despite the frustration of the July Revolution, we witness a series of revolutionary movements which we shall now cursorily review. We shall emphasise the events which in one way or another might have influenced the young Engels and Marx. In 1832 this movement was concentrated in southern Germany, not in the Rhine province, but in the Palatinate. Just like the Rhine province, the Palatinate was for a long time in the hands of France, for it was returned to Germany only after 1815. The Rhine province was handed over to Prussia, the Palatinate to Bavaria where reaction reigned not less than in Prussia. It can be readily understood why the inhabitants of the Rhine province and the Palatinate, who had been accustomed to the greater freedom of France, strongly resented German repression. Every revolutionary upheaval in France was bound to enhance opposition to the government. In 1831 this opposition assumed threatening proportions among the liberal intelligentsia, the lawyers and the writers of the Palatinate. In 1832, the lawyers Wirth and Ziebenpfeifer arranged a grand festival in Hambach. Many orators appeared on the rostrum. Börne too was present. They proclaimed the necessity of a free, united Germany. There was among them a very young man, Johann Philip Becker (1809-1886), brushmaker, who was about twenty-three years old. His name will be mentioned more than once in the course of this narrative. Becker tried to persuade the intelligentsia that they must not confine themselves to agitation, but that they must prepare for an armed insurrection. He was the typical revolutionist of the old school. An able man, he later became a writer, though he never became an outstanding theoretician. He was more the type of the practical revolutionist.

After the Hambach festivities, Becker remained in Germany for several years, his occupations resembling those of the Russian revolutionists of the seventies. He directed propaganda and agitation, arranged escapes and armed attacks to liberate comrades from prison. In this manner he aided quite a few revolutionists. In 1833 a group, with which Becker was closely connected (he himself was then in prison), made an attempt at an armed attack on the Frankfort guard-house, expecting to get hold of the arms. At that time the Diet was in session at Frankfort, and the students and workers were confident that having arranged a successful armed uprising they would create a furore throughout Germany. But they were summarily done away with. One of the most daring participants in this uprising was the previously mentioned Karl Schapper. He was fortunate in his escape back to France. It must be remembered that this entire movement was centred in localities which had for a long time been under French domination.

We must also note the revolutionary movement in the principality of Hesse. Here the leader was Weidig, a minister, a religious soul, but a fervent partisan of political freedom, and a fanatical worker for the cause of a United Germany. He established a secret printing press, issued revolutionary literature and endeavoured to attract the intelligentsia. One such intellectual who took a distinguished part in this movement was Georg Büchner (1813-1837), the

author of the drama, *The Death of Danton.* He differed
from Weidig in that in his political agitation he pointed
out the necessity of enlisting the sympathy of the Hessian
peasantry. He published a special propaganda paper for
the peasants—the first experiment of its kind—printed on
Weidig's press. Weidig was soon arrested and Büchner
escaped by a hair's breadth. He fled to Switzerland where
he died soon after. Weidig was incarcerated, and subjected
to corporal punishment. It might be mentioned that Weidig
was Wilhelm Liebknecht's uncle, and that the latter was
brought up under the influence of these profound impres-
sions.*

Some of the revolutionists freed from prison by Becker,
among whom were Schapper and Theodor Schuster, moved
to Paris and founded there a secret organisation called The
Society of the Exiles. Owing to the appearance of Schuster and other German workers who at that time settled in
Paris in great numbers, the Society took on a distinct
socialist character. This led to a split. One faction under
the guidance of Schuster formed the League of the Just,
which existed in Paris for three years.† Its members took
part in the Blanqui uprising, shared the fate of the Blanquists and landed in prison. When they were released,
Schapper and his comrades went to London. There they
organised the Workers' Educational Society, which was later
transformed into a communist organisation.‡

In the thirties there were quite a few other writers alongside of Börne who dominated the minds of the German intelligentsia. The most illustrious of them was Heinrich
Heine, the poet, who was also a publicist, and whose Paris
correspondence like the correspondence of Ludwig Börne,
was of great educational importance to the youth of Germany.

Börne and Heine were Jews. Börne came from the
Palatinate, Heine from the Rhine province where Marx

and Engels were born and grew up. Marx was also a Jew.

One of the questions that invariably presents itself is the extent to which Marx's subsequent fate was affected by the circumstances of his being a Jew.

The fact is that in the history of the German intelligentsia, in the history of German thought, four Jews played a monumental part. They were: Marx, Lassalle, Heine and Börne. More names could be enumerated, but these were the most notable. It must be stated that the fact that Marx as well as Heine were Jews had a good deal to do with the direction of their political development. If the university intelligentsia protested against the socio-political régime weighing upon Germany, then the Jewish intelligentsia felt this yoke even more keenly; one must read Börne to realise the rigours of the German censorship, one must read his articles in which he lashed philistine Germany and the police spirit that hovered over the land, to feel how a person, the least bit enlightened, could not help protesting against these abominations. The conditions were then particularly onerous for the Jew. Börne spent his entire youth in the Jewish district in Frankfort, under conditions very similar to those under which the Jews lived in the dark middle ages. Not less burdensome were these conditions to Heine.

Marx found himself in somewhat different circumstances. These, however, do not warrant the disposition of some biographers to deny this Jewish influence almost entirely.

Karl Marx was the son of Heinrich Marx, a lawyer, a highly educated, cultured and freethinking man. We know of Marx's father that he was a great admirer of the eighteenth-century literature of the French Enlightenment, and that altogether the French spirit seems to have pervaded the home of the Marxes. Marx's father liked to read, and interested his son in the writings of the English philosopher Locke, as well as the French writers Diderot and Voltaire.

Locke, one of the ideologists of the second so-called glorious English Revolution, was, in philosophy, the opponent of the principle of innate ideas. He instituted an inquiry into the origin of knowledge. Experience, he maintained, is the source of all we know; ideas are the result of experience; knowledge is wholly empirical; there are no innate ideas. The French materialists adopted the same position. They held that everything in the human mind reacted in one way or other through the sensory organs. The degree to which the atmosphere about Marx was permeated with the ideas of the French materialists can be judged from the following illustration.

Marx's father, who had long since severed all connections with religion, continued ostensibly to be bound up with Judaism. He adopted Christianity in 1824, when his son was already six years old. Franz Mehring (1846-1919) in his biography of Marx tried to prove that this conversion had been motivated by the elder Marx's determination to gain the right to enter the more cultured Gentile society. This is only partly true. The desire to avoid the new persecutions which fell upon the Jews since 1815, when the Rhine province was returned to Germany, must have had its influence.* We should note that Marx himself, though spiritually not in the least attached to Judaism, took a great interest in the Jewish question during his early years. He retained some contact with the Jewish community at Treves. In endless petitions the Jews had been importuning the government that one or another form of oppression be removed. In one case we know that Marx's close relatives and the rest of the Jewish community turned to him and asked him to write a petition for them. This happened when he was twenty-four years old.

All this indicates that Marx did not altogether shun his old kin, that he took an interest in the Jewish question and also a part in the struggle for the emancipation of the Jew.

This did not prevent him from drawing a sharp line of demarcation between poor Jewry with which he felt a certain propinquity and the opulent representatives of financial Jewry.

Treves, the city where Marx was born and where several of his ancestors were rabbis, was in the Rhine province. This was one of the Prussian provinces where industry and politics were in a high state of effervescence. Even now it is one of the most industrialised regions in Germany. There are Solingen and Remscheid, two cities famous for their steel products. There is the centre of the German textile industry—Barmen-Elberfeld. In Marx's home town, Treves, the leather and weaving industries were developed. It was an old mediæval city, which had played a big part in the tenth century. It was a second Rome, for it was the See of the Catholic bishop. It was also an industrial city, and during the French Revolution, it too was in the grip of a strong revolutionary paroxysm. The manufacturing industry, however, was here much less active than in the northern parts of the province, where the centres of the metallurgical and cotton industries were located. It lies on the banks of the Moselle, a tributary of the Rhine, in the centre of the wine manufacturing district, a place where remnants of communal ownership of land were still to be found, where the peasantry constituted a class of small landowners not yet imbued with the spirit of the tight-fisted, financially aggressive peasant-usurer, where they made wine and knew how to be happy. In this sense Treves preserved the traditions of the middle ages. From several sources we gather that at this time Marx was interested in the condition of the peasant. He would make excursions to the surrounding villages and thoroughly familiarise himself with the life of the peasant. A few years later he exhibited this knowledge of the details of peasant life and industry in his writings.

In high school Marx stood out as one of the most capable students, a fact of which the teachers took cognisance. We have a casual document in which a teacher made some very flattering comments on one of Karl's compositions. Marx was given an assignment to write a composition on "How Young Men Choose a Profession." He viewed this subject from a unique aspect. He proceeded to prove that there could be no free choice of a profession, that man was born into circumstances which predetermined his choice, for they moulded his *weltanschauung*. Here one may discern the germ of the Materialist Conception of History. After what was said of his father, however, it is obvious that in the above we have evidence of the degree to which Marx, influenced by his father, absorbed the basic ideas of the French materialists. It was the form in which the thought was embodied that was markedly original.

At the age of sixteen, Marx completed his high school course, and in 1835 he entered the University of Bonn. By this time revolutionary disturbances had well-nigh ceased. University life relapsed into its normal routine.

At the university, Marx plunged passionately into his studies.* We are in possession of a very curious document, a letter of the nineteen-year-old Marx to his father.

The father appreciated and understood his son perfectly. It is sufficient to read his reply to Marx to be convinced of the high degree of culture the man possessed. Rarely do we find in the history of revolutionists a case where a son meets with the full approval and understanding of his father, where a son turns to his father as to a very intimate friend. In accord with the spirit of the times, Marx was in search of a philosophy—a teaching which would enable him to give a theoretical foundation to the implacable hatred he felt for the then prevailing political and social system. Marx became a follower of the Hegelian philosophy, in the form which it had assumed with the Young Hegelians who had broken away most radically from old prejudices, and who through Hegel's philosophy had arrived at most extreme deductions in the realms of politics, civil and religious relations. In 1841 Marx obtained his doctorate from the University of Jena.*

At that time Engels too fell in with the set of the Young Hegelians. We do not know but that it was precisely in these circles that Engels first met Marx.†

Engels was born in Barmen, in the northern section of the Rhine province. This was the centre of the cotton and wool industries, not far from the future important metallurgical centre. Engels was of German extraction and belonged to a well-to-do family.

In the books containing genealogies of the merchants and the manufacturers of the Rhine province, the Engels family occupies a respectable place. Here one may find the family coat of arms of the Engelses. These merchants, not unlike the nobility, were sufficiently pedigreed to have their own coat of arms. Engels' ancestors bore on their shield an angel carrying an olive branch, the emblem of peace, signalising as it were, the pacific life and aspirations of one of the illustrious scions of their race. It is with this coat of arms that Engels entered life. This shield was most likely chosen because of the name, Engels, suggesting Angel in German. The prominence of this family can be judged by the fact that its origin can be traced back to the sixteenth century. As to Marx we can hardly ascertain who his grandfather was; all that is known is that his was a family of rabbis.‡ But so little interest had been taken in this family that records do not take us further back than two generations. Engels on the contrary has even two variants of his genealogy. According to certain data, Engels was a remote descendant of a Frenchman L'Ange, a Protestant, a Huguenot, who found refuge in Germany. Engels' more immediate relatives deny this French origin, insisting on his purely

German antecedents. At any rate, in the seventeenth century the Engels family was an old, firmly rooted family of cloth manufacturers, who later became cotton manufacturers. It was a wealthy family with extensive international dealings. The older Engels, together with his friend Erman, erected textile factories not only in his native land but also in Manchester. He became an Anglo-German textile manufacturer.

Engels' father belonged to the Protestant creed. An evangelist, he was curiously reminiscent of the old Calvinists, in his profound religious faith, and no less profound conviction, that the business of man on this earth is the acquisition and hoarding of wealth through industry and commerce. In life he was fanatically religious. Every moment away from business or other mundane activities he consecrated to pious reflections. On this ground the relations between the Engelses, father and son, were quite different from those we have observed in the Marx family. Very soon the ideas of father and son clashed; the father was resolved to make of his son a merchant, and he accordingly brought him up in the business spirit. At the age of seventeen the boy was sent to Bremen, one of the biggest commercial cities in Germany. There he was forced to serve in a business office for three years. By his letters to some school chums we learn how, having entered this atmosphere, Engels tried to free himself of its effects. He went there a godly youth, but soon fell under the sway of Heine and Börne. At the age of nineteen he became a writer and sallied forth as an apostle of a freedom-loving, democratic Germany. His first articles, which attracted attention and which appeared under the pseudonym of Oswald, mercilessly scored the environment in which the author had spent his childhood. These letters from Wupperthal created a strong impression. One could sense that they were written by a man who was brought up in that locality and who had a good knowledge of its people. While in Bremen he emancipated himself completely of all religious prepossessions and developed into an old French Jacobin.

About 1841, at the age of twenty, Engels entered the Artillery Guards of Berlin as a volunteer. There he fell in with the same circle of the Young Hegelians to which Marx belonged. He became the adherent of the extreme left wing of the Hegelian philosophy. While Marx, in 1842, was still engrossed in his studies and was preparing himself for a University career, Engels, who had begun to write in 1839, attained a conspicuous place in literature under his old pseudonym, and was taking a most active part in the ideological struggles which were carried on by the disciples of the old and the new philosophical systems.

In the years 1841 and 1842 there lived in Berlin a great number of Russians—Bakunin, Ogarev, Frolov and others. They too were fascinated by the same philosophy which fascinated Marx and Engels. To what extent this is true can be shown by the following episode. In 1842 Engels wrote a trenchant criticism of the philosophy of Hegel's adversary, Friedrich Schelling. The latter then received an invitation from the Prussian government to come to Berlin and to pit his philosophy, which endeavoured to reconcile the Bible with science, against the Hegelian system.* The views expressed by Engels at that period were so suggestive of the views of the Russian critic Bielinsky of that period, and of the articles of Bakunin, that, up to very recently, Engels' pamphlet in which he had attacked Schelling's *Philosophy of Revelation,* was ascribed to Bakunin. Now we know that it was an error, that the pamphlet was not written by Bakunin. The forms of expression of both writers, the subjects they chose, the proofs they presented while attempting to establish the perfections of the Hegelian philosophy, were so remarkably similar that it is little wonder that many Russians considered and still consider Bakunin the author of this booklet.

Thus at the age of twenty-two, Engels was an accomplished democratic writer, with ultra-radical tendencies. In one of his humorous poems he depicted himself a fiery Jacobin. In this respect he reminds one of those few Germans who had become very much attached to the French Revolution. According to himself, all he sang was the Marseillaise, all he clamoured for was the guillotine. Such was Engels in the year 1842. Marx was in about the same mental state. In 1842 they finally met in one common cause.

Marx was graduated from the university and received his doctor's degree in April, 1841. He had proposed at first to devote himself to philosophy and science, but he gave up this idea when his teacher and friend, Bruno Bauer, who was one of the leaders of the Young Hegelians lost his right to teach at the university because of his severe criticism of the official theology.

It was a case of good fortune for Marx to be invited at this time to edit a newspaper. Representatives of the more radical commercial-industrial bourgeoisie of the Rhine province had made up their minds to found their own political organ. The most important newspaper in the Rhine province was the *Kölnische Zeitung*, and Cologne was then the greatest industrial centre of the Rhine district. The *Kölnische Zeitung* cringed before the government. The Rhine radical bourgeoisie wanted their own organ to oppose the *Kölnische Zeitung* and to defend their economic interests against the feudal lords. Money was collected, but there was a dearth of literary forces. Journals founded by capitalists fell into the hands of a group of radical writers. Above them all towered Moses Hess (1812-1875). Moses Hess was older than either Engels or Marx. Like Marx he was a Jew, but he very early broke away from his rich father. He soon joined the movement for liberation, and even as far back as the thirties, advocated the formation of a league of the cultured nations in order to insure the winning of political and cultural freedom. In 1842, influenced by the French communist movement, Moses Hess became a communist. It was he and his friends who were among the prominent editors of the *Rheinische Zeitung*.

Marx lived then in Bonn. For a long time he was only a contributor, though he had already begun to wield considerable influence. Gradually Marx rose to a position of first magnitude. Thus, though the newspaper was published at the expense of the Rhine industrial middle class, in reality it became the organ of the Berlin group of the youngest and most radical writers.

In the autumn of 1842 Marx moved to Cologne and immediately gave the journal an entirely new trend. In contradistinction to his Berlin comrades, as well as Engels, he insisted on a less noisy yet more radical struggle against the existing political and social conditions. Unlike Engels, Marx, as a child, had never felt the goading yoke of religious and intellectual oppression—a reason why he was rather indifferent to the religious struggle, why he did not deem it necessary to spend all his strength on a bitter criticism of religion. In this respect he preferred polemics about essentials to polemics about mere externals. Such a policy was indispensable, he thought, to preserve the paper as a radical organ. Engels was much nearer to the group that demanded relentless open war against religion. A similar difference of opinion existed among the Russian revolutionists towards the end of 1917 and the beginning of 1918. Some demanded an immediate and sweeping attack upon the Church. Others maintained that this was not essential, that there were more serious problems to tackle. The disagreement between Marx, Engels and other young publicists was of the same nature. Their controversy found expression in the epistles which Marx as editor sent to his old comrades in

Berlin. Marx stoutly defended his tactics. He emphasised the question of the wretched conditions of the labouring masses. He subjected to the most scathing criticism the laws which prohibited the free cutting of timber. He pointed out that the spirit of these laws was the spirit of the propertied and landowning class who used all their ingenuity to exploit the peasants, and who purposely devised ordinances that would render the peasants criminals. In his correspondence he took up the cudgels for his old acquaintances, the Moselle peasants. These articles provoked a caustic controversy with the governor of the Rhine province.

The local authorities brought pressure to bear at Berlin. A double censorship was imposed upon the paper. Since the authorities felt that Marx was the soul of the paper, they insisted on his dismissal. The new censor had great respect for this intelligent and brilliant publicist, who so dexterously evaded the censorship obstacles, but he nevertheless continued to inform against Marx not only to the editorial management, but also to the group of stockholders who were behind the paper. Among the latter, the feeling began to grow that greater caution and the avoidance of all kinds of embarrassing questions would be the proper policy to pursue. Marx refused to acquiesce. He asserted that any further attempt at moderation would prove futile, that at any rate the government would not be so easily pacified. Finally he resigned his editorship and left the paper. This did not save the paper, for it soon was forced to discontinue.

Marx left the paper a completely transformed man. He had entered the newspaper not at all a communist. He had simply been a radical democrat, interested in the social and economic conditions of the peasantry. But he gradually became more and more absorbed in the study of the basic economic problems relating to the peasant question. From philosophy and jurisprudence Marx was drawn into a detailed and specialised study of economic relations.

In addition, a new polemic between Marx and a conservative journal burst out in connection with an article written by Hess who, in 1842, converted Engels to communism. Marx vehemently denied the paper's right to attack communism. "I do not know communism," he said, "but a social philosophy that has as its aim the defence of the oppressed cannot be condemned so lightly. One must acquaint himself thoroughly with this trend of thought ere he dares dismiss it." When Marx left the *Rheinische Zeitung* he was not yet a communist, but he was already interested in communism as a particular tendency representing a particular point of view. Finally, he and his friend, Arnold Ruge (1802-1880), came to the conclusion that there was no possibility for conducting political and social propaganda in Germany. They decided to go to Paris (1843) and there publish a journal *Deutsch-Französischen Jahrbücher* (Franco-German Year Books). By this name they wanted, in contradistinction to the French and German nationalists, to emphasise that one of the conditions of a successful struggle against reaction was a close political alliance between Germany and France. In the *Jahrbücher* [1] Marx formulated for the first time the basic principles of his future philosophy, in which evolution of a radical democrat into a communist is discerned.

[1] Only two issues were published, both appearing in 1844.

CHAPTER III

THIS study of the lives of Marx and Engels is in accordance with the scientific method they themselves developed and employed.   Despite their genius, Marx and Engels were after all men of a definite historic moment.   As both of them matured, that is, as both of them gradually emerged from their immediate home influence they were directly drawn into the vortex of the historic epoch which was characterised chiefly by the effects upon Germany of the July Revolution, by the forward strides of science and philosophy, by the growth of the labour and the revolutionary movements. Marx and Engels were not only the products of a definite historic period, but in their very origin they were men of a specific locality, the Rhine province, which of all parts of Germany was the most international, the most industrialised, and the most widely exposed to the influence of the French Revolution.   During the first years of his life, Marx was subjected to different influences than Engels, while the Marx family was under the sway of the French materialists, Engels was brought up in a religious, almost sanctimonious, atmosphere.   This was reflected in their later development.   Questions pertaining to religion never touched Marx so painfully and so profoundly as they did Engels.   Finally, both, though by different paths, one by an easier one, the other by a more tortuous one, arrived at the same conclusions.

We have now reached the point in the careers of these

two men when they become the exponents of the most radical political and philosophical thought of the period. It was in the *Deutsch-Französischen Jahrbücher* that Marx formulated his new point of view. That we may grasp what was really new in the conception of the twenty-five-year-old Marx, let us first hastily survey what Marx had found in the realm of philosophy.

In a preface (Sept. 21, 1882) to his *Socialism, Utopian and Scientific*, Engels wrote: "We German socialists are proud that we trace our descent not only from Saint Simon, Fourier and Owen, but also from Kant, Fichte and Hegel." Engels does not mention Ludwig Feuerbach, though he later devoted a special work to this philosopher. We shall now proceed to study the philosophic origin of scientific socialism.

One of the fundamental problems of metaphysics is the question of a first cause, a First Principle, a something antecedent to mundane existence—that which we are in the habit of calling God. This Creator, this Omnipotent and Omnipresent One, may assume different forms in different religions. He may manifest Himself in the image of an almighty heavenly monarch, with countless angels as His messenger boys. He may relegate His power to popes, bishops and priests. Or, as an enlightened and good monarch, He may grant once for all a constitution, establish fundamental laws whereby everything human and natural shall be ruled and, without interfering in the affairs of government, or ever getting mixed up in any other business, be satisfied with the love and reverence of His children. He may, in short, reveal Himself in the greatest variety of forms. But once we recognise the existence of this God and these little gods, we thereby admit the existence of some divine being who, on waking one beautiful morning, uttered, "Let there be a world!" and a world sprung into being. Thus the thought, the will, the intention to create our world existed somewhere outside of it. We cannot be any more specific as to its whereabouts, for the secret has not yet been revealed to us by any philosopher.

This primary entity creates all being. The idea creates matter; consciousness determines all being. In its essence, despite its philosophic wrappings, this new form of the manifestation of the First Principle is a recrudescence of the old theology. It is the same Lord of Sabaoth, or Father or Son or Holy Ghost. Some even call it Reason, or the Word, or Logos. "At the beginning was the Word." The Word created Being. The Word created the world.

The conception that "At the beginning was the Word," aroused the opposition of the eighteenth-century materialists. Insofar as they attacked the old social order—the feudal system—these represented a new view, a new class— the revolutionary bourgeoisie. The old philosophy did not provide an answer to the question as to how the new, which undoubtedly distinguished their time from the old time—the new ages from the preceding ones—originated.

Mind, idea, reason—these had one serious flaw, they were static, permanent, unalterable. But experience showed the mutability of everything earthly. Being was embodied in the most variegated forms. History as well as contemporary life, travel and discoveries, revealed a world so rich, so multiform and so fluid that in the face of all this a static philosophy could not survive.

The crucial question therefore was: Wherefrom all this multifariousness? Where did this complexity arise? How did these subtle differentiations in time and space originate? How could one primary cause—God the eternal and unalterable—be the cause of these numberless changes? The naïve supposition that all these were mere whims of God could satisfy no one any more.

Beginning with the eighteenth century, though it was already strongly perceptible in the seventeenth, human relations were going through precipitous changes, and as these changes were themselves the result of human activity, Deity as the ultimate source of everything began to inspire ever graver doubts. For that which explains everything, in all its multifariousness, both in time and in space, does not really explain anything. It is not what is common to all things, but the differences between things that can be explained only by the presumption that things are different because they were created under different circumstances, under the influence of different causes. Every such difference must be explained by particular, specific causes, by particular influences which produced it.

The English philosophers, having been exposed to the effects of a rapidly expanding capitalism and the experiences of two revolutions, boldly questioned the actual existence of a superhuman force responsible for all these events. Also the conception of man's innate ideas emanating from one First Principle appeared extremely dubious in view of the diversity of new and conflicting ideas which were crystallised during the period of revolution.

The French materialists propounded the same question, but even more boldly. They denied the existence of an extra-mundane divine power which was constantly preoccupied with the affairs of the New Europe, and which was busy shaping the destinies of everything and everybody. To them everything observable in man's existence, in man's history, was the result of man's own activity.

The French materialists could not point out or explain what determined human action. But they were firm in their knowledge that neither God nor any other external power made history. Herein lay a contradiction which they could not reconcile. They knew that men act differently, because of different interests and different opinions. The cause of these differences in interests and opinions they could not discern. Of course, they ascribed these to differences in education and bringing up; which was true. But what de-

termined the type of education and bringing up? Here the
French materialists failed. The nature of society, of education, etc., was in their opinion, determined by laws made by
men, by legislators, by lawgivers. Thus the lawmaker is
elevated into the position of an arbiter and director of human
action. In his powers he is almost a God. And what determines the action of the lawgiver? This they did not
know.

One more question was being thrashed out at this time.
Some of the philosophers of the early French Enlightenment
were Deists. "Of course," they maintained, "our Deity does
not in any way resemble the cruel Hebrew God, nor the
Father, the Son and the Holy Ghost of the Christian creed.
Yet we feel that there is a spiritual principle, which im-
pregnated matter with the very ability to think, a supreme
power which antedated nature." The materialists' answer
to this was that there was no need for postulating an external power, and that sensation is the natural attribute
of matter.

Science in general, and the natural sciences in particular,
were not yet sufficiently advanced when the French materialists tried to work out their views. Without having positive
proof they nevertheless arrived at the fundamental proposition mentioned above.

Every materialist rejects the consciousness—the mind—as
antecedent to matter and to nature. For thousands, nay
millions, of years there was not an intimation of a living,
organic being upon this planet, that is, there was not anything here of what is called mind or consciousness. Existence, nature, matter preceded consciousness, preceded spirit
and mind.

One must not think, however, that Matter is necessarily
something crude, cumbrous, unclean, while the Idea is something delicate, ethereal and pure. Some, particularly the
vulgar materialists and, at times, simply young people, un-

wittingly assert in the heat of argument and often to spite
the Pharisees of idealism, who only prate of the "lofty and
the beautiful" while adapting themselves most comfortably
to the filth and meanness of their bourgeois surroundings,
that matter is something ponderous and crude.

This, of course, is a mistaken view. For a hundred and
fifty years we have been learning that matter is incredibly
ethereal and mobile. Ever since the Industrial Revolution
has turned the abutments of the old and sluggish natural
economy upside down, things began to move. The dormant
was awakened; the motionless was stirred into activity. In
hard, seemingly frozen matter new forces were discovered and
new kinds of motion discerned.

How inadequate was the knowledge of the French materialists, can be judged from the following. When d'Holbach,
for instance, was writing his *System of Nature*, he knew less
of the essential nature of phenomena than an elementary
school graduate to-day. Air to him was a primary element. He knew as little about air as the Greeks had known
two thousand years before him. Only a few years after
d'Holbach had written his chief work, chemistry proved
that air was a mixture of a variety of elements—nitrogen,
oxygen and others. A hundred years later, towards the
end of the nineteenth century, chemistry discovered in the
air the rare gases, argon, helium, etc. Matter, to be sure!
But not so very crude.

Another instance. Nowadays we all use the radio and
wireless most diligently. It renders us great services. Without it we would literally be groping in the dark. Yet a
study of its development shows us its comparatively recent
origin—about twenty-five years. It was only in 1897 or
1898 that matter revealed to us such unmaterial attributes
that we had to turn to Hindoo theology to find terms to
depict them.* The radio transmits signs and sounds. One
may be in Moscow and enjoy a concert broadcast a few

thousand miles away. It is only very recently that we have learned that even photographs can be transmitted by radio. All these miracles are performed not through some "spiritual" agency, but by means of very ethereal, and, no doubt, very delicate, but none the less quite measurable and controllable matter.

The above examples were adduced for the purpose of illustrating the obsoleteness of some conceptions of the material and the immaterial. They were even more obsolete in the eighteenth century. Had the materialists of those days had at their disposal all the recently disclosed facts, they would not have been so "crude," and they would not have offended the "sensibilities" of some people.

Immanuel Kant's (1724-1804) contemporaries among the German philosophers held to the orthodox point of view. They rejected materialism as godless and immoral. Kant, however, was not satisfied with such a simple solution. He knew full well the flimsiness of the traditional religious notions. But he had neither enough courage nor enough consistency definitely to break with the old.

In 1781 he published his magnum opus the *Critique of Pure Reason* in which he established most conclusively that all knowledge was empirical, and that there were no proofs for the existence of a God, the immortality of the soul, absolute ideas, etc. We do not know things in themselves, their essences. We can know only the forms in which these essences manifest themselves to our sensory organs. The essence of things (noumenon) is concealed behind the form (phenomenon) and it will forever remain in the realm of the unknown. It appeared that the gulf between materialism and idealism, between science and religion was bridged. Kant did not deny the successes of science in the study and the explanation of phenomena. But he also found a place for theology. The essence was christened with the name of God.

In his double-entry system of bookkeeping, in his determination to offend neither science nor religion, Kant went even further. In his next work, the *Critique of Practical Reason*, he proceeded to prove that though in theory the conceptions God, immortality of the soul, etc., are not indispensable, in practice one is forced to accept them, for without them human activity would be devoid of any moral basis.

The poet Heine, who was a friend of Marx and upon whom the latter at one time had a great influence, depicted very vividly Kant's motives for treading the two paths. Kant had an old and faithful servant, Lampe, who had lived with, and attended to, his master for forty years. For Kant this Lampe was the personification of the average man who could not live without religion. After a brilliant exposition of the revolutionary import of the *Critique of Pure Reason* in the struggle with theology and with the belief in a Divine Principle, Heine explained why Kant found it necessary to write the *Critique of Practical Reason* in which the philosopher re-established everything he had torn down before. Here is what Heine wrote:

"After the tragedy comes the farce. Immanuel Kant has hitherto appeared as the grim, inexorable philosopher; he has stormed heaven, put all the garrison to the sword; the ruler of the world swims senseless in his blood; there is no more any mercy, or fatherly goodness, or future reward for present privations; the immortality of the soul is in its last agonies—death rattles and groans. And old Lampe stands by with his umbrella under his arm as a sorrowing spectator, and the sweat of anguish and tears run down his cheeks. Then Immanuel Kant is moved to pity, and shows himself not only a great philosopher, but a good man. He reconsiders, and half good-naturedly and half ironically says, 'Old Lampe must have a God, or else the poor man cannot be happy, and people really ought to be happy in this world. Practical common sense declares that. Well,

meinet wegen, for all I care, let practical reason guarantee
the existence of a God.' " [1]

Kant had a great influence on science, too. Together
with the French astronomer Pierre Laplace (1749-1827),
he maintained that the biblical account of the creation of
the world was faulty, that the earth was the product of a
prolonged development, of a continuous evolutionary process, that like all heavenly bodies it came about as the gradual
congealment of a highly rarefied substance.

Kant was essentially a mediator between the old and the
new philosophies; he remained a compromiser in most practical fields of life. Though he was not able completely to
break away from the old, he none the less made a considerable step forward. His more consistent disciples rejected
the *Critique of Practical Reason* and made the most extreme
deductions from his *Critique of Pure Reason.*

The philosopher Johann Fichte (1762-1814) impressed
Lassalle incomparably more than he did Marx or Engels.
But there was one element in his philosophy which was absolutely neglected in the Kantian system and which had a
tremendous influence upon the German revolutionary intelligentsia. Kant was a peaceful professor. Not once in a few
decades was he even tempted to go beyond the boundaries
of his beloved Königsberg. Fichte, on the contrary, besides
being a philosopher, was active in the practical pursuits of
life. It was this element of action that Fichte carried over
into his philosophy. To the old conception of an external
power that directed the actions of men, he opposed the idea
of the Absolute Ego, thus converting the human personality
and its activity into the mainspring of all theory and practice.

Yet it was G. W. F. Hegel (1770-1831) who, more than
any other philosopher, exerted a powerful influence on Marx

[1] Heinrich Heine, Collected Works. W. Heineman, London, 1906.
Vol. 5, pp. 150-151.

and Engels. His philosophy was based on a criticism of the Kantian and Fichtean systems. In his youth Hegel had been an ardent devotee of the French Revolution, while toward the end of his life he became a Prussian professor and official, and his philosophy was most graciously approved of by the "enlightened" rulers.

The question then presents itself how was it that Hegel's philosophy became the source of inspiration for Marx, Engels and Lassalle. What was it in Hegel's philosophy that irresistibly drew to itself the most illustrious exponents of social and revolutionary thought?

Kant's philosophy, in its main outlines, had taken shape previous to the French Revolution. He was sixty-five years old when the Revolution began. True, he, too, was moved sympathetically, still he never went further than his customary compromising and conciliatory deductions. Though with regard to the history of our planet, as we have seen, he had already adopted the idea of evolution, his philosophic system, nevertheless, reduced itself to an explanation of the universe as it was.

With Hegel it was different. Having gone through the experiences of the late eighteenth and the early nineteenth century, that epoch of colossal economic and political changes, he viewed and explained the cosmos as a continuous process of unfoldment. There is nothing immobile. The Absolute Idea lives and manifests itself only in the process of uninterrupted movement—development. Everything flows, changes and vanishes. The ceaseless movement, the eternal unfoldment of the Absolute Idea determines the evolution of the world in all its aspects. To comprehend the circumambient phenomena, one must not only study them as they exist, but one must understand how they have been developing; for everything about one is the result of a past development. Furthermore, a thing may appear at first glance as being in a state of immobility which on closer scrutiny, however, will disclose within itself incessant movement and conflict, numerous influences and forces, some tending to preserve it as it is, others tending to change it. In each phenomenon, in each object, there is the clash of two principles, the *thesis* and the *antithesis*, the conservative and the destructive. This struggle between the two opposing principles resolves itself into a final harmonious *synthesis* of the two.

This is how it was expressed in the Hegelian idiom. The Reason, the Thought, the Idea, does not remain motionless; it does not remain frozen to one proposition; it does not remain on the same thesis. On the contrary, the thesis, the thought interposing itself breaks up into two contradictory ideas, a positive and a negative, a "yes" idea, and a "no" idea. The conflict between the two contradictory elements included in the antithesis creates movement, which Hegel, in order to underline the element of conflict, styles *dialectic*. The result of this conflict, this dialectic, is reconciliation, or equilibrium. The fusion of the two opposite ideas forms a new idea, their synthesis. This in its turn divides into two contradictory ideas—the thesis is converted into its antithesis, and these again are blended in a new synthesis.

Hegel regarded every phenomenon as a process, as something that is forever changing, something that is forever developing. Every phenomenon is not only the result of previous changes, it also carries within itself the germ of future changes. It never halts at any stage. The equilibrium attained is disturbed by a new conflict, which leads to a higher reconciliation, to a higher synthesis, and to a still further dichotomy on a still higher plane. Thus, it is the struggle between opposites that is the source of all development.

Herein lay the revolutionary potentialities of Hegel's philosophy. Though he was an idealist, though his system was based on the Spirit and not on Nature, on the Idea and not on Matter, he none the less exerted a great influence upon all historical and social sciences, and even upon natural science. He stimulated the study of reality. He inspired the study of the various forms which the Absolute Idea had assumed in the process of its unfoldment. And the more variegated were the forms through which the Idea manifested itself, the more variegated were the phenomena and the processes that had to be investigated.

We shall not dwell on the other sides of the Hegelian philosophy which would make clear why it gave such a powerful impulse for a more careful study of reality. The more his disciples studied reality in the light of and guided by, the dialectic method evolved by their teacher, the more evident became the radical deficiency of his philosophy. For it was an idealistic philosophy; that is, the motivating force, the Creator, was, according to Hegel, the Absolute Idea, which determined existence. This weak point in the Hegelian system called forth criticism. The Absolute Idea seemed a new edition of the old God, the same bodiless God which such philosophers as Voltaire created for themselves and particularly for the masses.

Ludwig Feuerbach (1804-1872), one of the most talented disciples of Hegel, finally examined his master's philosophy from this point of view. He understood perfectly and mastered the revolutionary aspect of the Hegelian System. He propounded, however, the following question: Can the Absolute Idea in its development actually determine all being? To this question Feuerbach gave a negative answer. He upset Hegel's basic proposition by pointing out the converse to be the truth—Being determines Consciousness. There was a time when there was being without consciousness. The Mind or the Idea is itself the product of Being. He regarded Hegel's philosophy as the latest theological system, for in place of a God, it conjured up another primary Being, the Absolute Idea. Feuerbach indicated that the various conceptions of God, Christianity included, were created by man himself. Not God had created man, but rather man created

God, in his own image. It is merely necessary to dissipate this world of phantoms, occult objects, angels, witches and similar manifestations of the basically same Divine Essence, to have left a human world. Thus Man becomes the fundamental principle of Feuerbach's philosophy. The supreme law in this human world is not the law of God but the happiness of man. In opposition to the old theological Deistic principle, Feuerbach advanced a new anthropological or human principle.

In his school composition, mentioned in an earlier chapter, Marx had claimed that by a chain of circumstances operative even before a man's birth, his future profession is predetermined. Thus the idea which followed logically from the materialist philosophy of the eighteenth century was familiar to Marx when he was yet at high school. Man is the product of his environment, and of conditions; he cannot therefore be free in the choice of his profession, he cannot be the maker of his own happiness. There was nothing new or original in this view. Marx was merely formulating in a unique manner, to be sure, what he had already read in the works of the philosophers to which he had been introduced by his father. When he entered the University and came in touch with the classical German philosophy that was reigning there, he began from the very first to expound a materialist philosophy in opposition to the then prevailing idealistic thought. This was why he so soon arrived at the most radical deductions from the Hegelian system. This was also why he greeted so warmly Feuerbach's *Essence of Christianity*. In his criticism of Christianity, Feuerbach came to the same conclusions to which the eighteenth-century materialists had come. But where they had seen only deceit and bigotry, he, who had gone through the Hegelian school, discerned a necessary phase of human culture. But even to Feuerbach, man was as much of an abstract figure as he was to the materialists of the eighteenth century.

It was necessary to go only one step further in the analysis of man and his surroundings to discover that man was quite varied, existing in diverse spheres, having a different status. The Prussian king, the Moselle peasant, as well as the factory worker, whom Marx had been meeting in the Rhine province, were all men. They all had the same organs—heads, feet, hands, etc. Physiologically and anatomically there was not any great difference between the Moselle peasant and the Prussian landlord. Yet there was an overwhelming difference in their social position. Futhermore, men differed from each other not only in space but in time, those of the seventeenth century differing from those of the twelfth, and from those of the nineteenth. How did all these differences originate, if man himself was not changing, if he was exclusively a product of nature?

Marx's thought began to work in this direction. To maintain that man is the product of his environment, that he is fashioned by his surroundings, is not enough. To breed such differences, environment itself must be a complex of contradictions. Environment is not a mere collection of people, it is rather a social milieu in which men are bound up in definite relations and belong to distinct social groups.

This was why Marx could not be satisfied even with Feuerbach's critique of religion. Feuerbach explained the essence of religion by the essence of man. But the essence of man is not at all something abstract and belonging to man as a separate individual. Man himself represents an aggregate, a totality of definite social relations. There is no separated and isolated man. Even the *natural* ties existing among men recede before the significance of social ties that are established in the process of historical development. Therefore religious sentiment is not anything natural, but is itself a *social* product.

The assertion that man is the source of a new *weltanschauung* seems inadequate. One must emphasise the social aspect in the concept of man. One must think of man as the product of a certain social development who is formed and brought up upon a definite social soil specifically stratified and differentiated. This stratification and differentiation of the environment into distinct classes is not anything primordial, but is the result of a long developmental process. An investigation of the manner in which this historical process was accomplished shows that it has always resulted from a struggle between opposites, between contradictions that had appeared at a certain definite stage of social development.

Marx did not confine himself to this, he subjected to his criticism other propositions of Feuerbach's philosophy. Into the purely theoretical contemplative philosophy he injected a new revolutionary element which was based on a criticism of reality—practical activity.

Like the French materialists, Feuerbach taught that man was the product of circumstances and education, the product of existence acting upon consciousness. Thus man as he is, with his head, hands, feet, etc., and set apart from the animal kingdom, was viewed as a sort of sensitive apparatus subjected to the influences and the action of nature upon him. All his thoughts, his ideas, are reflections of nature. According to Feuerbach it seemed, therefore, that man was a purely passive element, an obedient recipient of impulses supplied by nature.

To this proposition Marx opposed another. Everything, he insisted, that goes on within man, the changes of man himself, are the effects not only of the influence of nature upon man, but even more so of the reaction of man upon nature. It is this that constitutes the evolution of man. The primitive manlike animal in his eternal struggle for existence did not merely passively subject himself to the stimuli that came from nature, he reacted upon nature, he changed it. Having changed nature, he changed the conditions of his existence—he also changed himself.

Thus Marx introduced a revolutionary, active element into Feuerbach's passive philosophy. The business of philosophy, maintained Marx in contradistinction to Feuerbach, is not only to explain this world, but also to change it. Theory should be supplemented by practice. The critique of facts, of the world about us, the negation of them, should be supplemented by positive work and by practical activity. Thus had Marx converted Feuerbach's contemplative philosophy into an active one. By our whole activity must we prove the correctness of our thought and our programme. The more efficiently we introduce our ideas into practice, the sooner we embody them in actuality, the more indubitable is the proof that actuality had in it the elements that were needed for the solution of the problem we had confronted ourselves with, for the execution of the programme we had worked out.

The general features of this criticism of Feuerbach were formulated by Marx at quite an early period. A thoughtful examination of the line of his thought shows how he arrived at his fundamental idea the elaboration of which led him to scientific communism.

In his polemics with the German intelligentsia, from whose midst he had himself emerged, Marx tried to prove the bankruptcy of their old slogans.

We all agree, he told them, that the German reality about us, the Prussia where life is so difficult, where there is neither freedom of thought nor teaching, presents in itself something utterly unattractive. There is not the slightest doubt that this world must be changed, if we do not wish the German people to sink to the bottom of this horrible morass.

But how can this world be changed? inquired Marx. This change is contingent upon the presence within German so-

ciety of some group, a category of people, who would
with every fibre of their being be interested in bringing
about the change.

Marx examined successively the various groups existing
within German society—the nobility, the bureaucracy, the
bourgeoisie. He came to the conclusion that even the last
mentioned, unlike the French bourgeoisie which played such
an important revolutionary part, was not capable of taking
upon itself the rôle of the "liberator class" which would
completely change the social system.

If not the bourgeoisie, which other class would measure
up to the task? And Marx who was at that time steeped
in the study of the histories and the prevailing condition of
France and England, concluded that the *proletariat* was
the only class that held out any real social promise.

Thus even in 1844, Marx advanced his main thesis: *The
class that is capable and that should assume the mission of
freeing the German people and of changing the social order
is the proletariat. . . . Why?* Because it constitutes a class
of people whose very conditions of existence are the embodi-
ment of what is most pernicious in contemporary bourgeois
society. No other class stands as low on the social ladder,
feels as heavily the weight of the rest of society. While
the existence of all the other classes of society is founded
upon private property, the proletariat is devoid of this
property and consequently not in the least interested in the
preservation of the present order. The proletariat, however,
lacks the consciousness of its mission, lacks knowledge and
philosophy. It will become the propeller of the entire emancipation movement once it becomes imbued with this consciousness, this philosophy, once it understands the conditions requisite for its emancipation, once it conceives the
exalted rôle that fell to its lot.

This point of view is exclusively Marxian. The
great Utopian Socialists—Claude Saint-Simon (1760-1825),

Charles Fourier (1772-1837), and particularly Robert Owen (1771-1858)—had already directed their attention to the "most numerous and the neediest class"—the proletarians. But they worked on the assumptions that the proletariat was merely the most suffering class, the most indigent class, that it had to be taken care of, and that this care had to be exercised by the higher, cultured classes. In the poverty of the proletariat they saw only poverty, they did not fathom the revolutionary possibilities immanent in this poverty, the product of the decay of bourgeois society.

Marx was the first to point out that the proletariat besides being merely the suffering class, was the active fighter against the bourgeois order; it was the class which in every condition of its existence was being converted into the sole revolutionary element in bourgeois society.

This idea, advanced by Marx at the beginning of 1844, was further developed by him in collaboration with Engels in a work called *The Holy Family*.* Though a bit obsolete, this book is not much more obsolete than some of the early works of Plekhanov or of Lenin. It is still full of interest to those who are aware of the intense intellectual and social struggles that were raging in Germany in the early forties. In this book Marx vehemently ridicules all the attempts of the German intelligentsia either to turn away from the proletariat, or to find satisfaction in philanthropic societies which were expected greatly to benefit the proletariat. Marx again tried to explain to the German intelligentsia the revolutionary significance of the proletariat, which only a few months before had shown, by the uprisings of the Silesian weavers, that when it came to a defence of its material interests the proletariat did not stop at insurrection.

Marx was already adumbrating in this book the guideposts of his new philosophy. The proletariat is a distinct class, for the society in which it lives is constructed on class lines. The proletariat is opposed by the bourgeoisie. The worker is exploited by the capitalist. There is still another question. Where did the capitalists come from? What were the causes that engendered this exploitation of hired labour by capital?

There was need for a scientific examination of the fundamental laws of this society, its evolution and its existence. In this book Marx already stressed the importance of a knowledge of the conditions of industry, of production, of the material conditions of life, of the relations established among people in the process of satisfying their material wants, for a thorough comprehension of the real forces working in any given historic period.

From then on Marx began to work assiduously upon this problem. He threw himself into the study of political economy to clarify for himself the mechanism of economic relations in contemporary society. But Marx was not only a philosopher who wanted to explain the world, he was also a revolutionist who wanted to change it.

CHAPTER IV

WE shall now proceed to examine the extent to which Marx took part in the organization of the Communist League at the request of which the *Communist Manifesto* was written. After examining all the data obtainable from the writings of Marx and Engels pertaining to this question, one must conclude that their account regarding the origin of the League is not entirely correct. Marx had occasion to touch upon this episode only once in one of his works that is read very little, *Herr Vogt*, published in 1860. He allowed a great number of errors to creep into that book. The history of the Communist League is usually learned through the account written by Engels in 1885. Engels' story can be summarised as follows:*

Once there lived Marx and Engels, two German philosophers and politicians, who were forced to abandon their native land. They lived in France and they lived in Belgium. They wrote learned books, which first attracted the attention of the intelligentsia, and then fell into the hands of the workers. One fine morning the workers turned to these two savants who had been sitting in their cloisters remote from the loathsome business of practical activity and, as was proper for guardians of scientific thought, had been proudly awaiting the coming of the workers. And the day arrived; the workers came and invited Marx and Engels to enter their League. But Marx and Engels declared that they would join the League only on condition that the League accept their programme. The workers agreed, they organized the Communist League and forthwith proceeded to authorise Marx and Engels to prepare the *Communist Manifesto.*

The workers who did this had belonged to the League of the Just which was mentioned in connection with the history of the labour movement in France and England. It was pointed out that this League of the Just had been formed in Paris and that it had suffered serious reverses after the unsuccessful uprising of the Blanquists on May 12, 1839. It was also reported that after the defeat, the members of the League went to London. Among them was Schapper who organised the Workers' Educational Society in February, 1840.

U. Steklov, in his book on Marx, gives a similar account of the origin of the Communist League.*

"While living in Paris, Marx was keeping in personal touch with the leaders of the League of the Just which consisted of German political emigrants and artisans. He did not join this League because its programme was too greatly coloured with an idealistic and conspiratory spirit which could not appeal to Marx. The rank and file of the League, however, gradually came to a position approaching that of Marx and Engels. The latter through personal and written contact, as well as through the press, influenced the political views of the members of the League. On some occasions the two friends transmitted their views to their correspondents through printed circulars. After the breach with the rebel Weitling, after the systematically 'severe criticism of the useless theoreticians,' the soil was fully prepared for Marx and Engels to join the League. At the first congress of the League, which had now assumed the name of the Communist League, Engels and Wilhelm Wolff were present; at the second convention, at the end of November, 1847, Marx, too, was present. The convention, after having heard

Marx's address in which he expounded the new socialist philosophy, commissioned him and Engels to prepare the programme of the League. This was how the famous *Communist Manifesto* came to be written."

Steklov has only related what Marx had written, while Mehring has repeated what Engels had told us. And one cannot but believe Engels, for who is more qualified to relate the history of an enterprise than the person who himself took part in it? Still a critical attitude must be preserved even where Engels is concerned, particularly since in his article he described affairs that had occurred forty years before. After such a considerable interval of time it is rather easy to forget things, particularly if one writes under entirely different circumstances and in a wholly different mood.

We have at our disposal other facts which do not at all tally with the above account. Marx and Engels were not at all the pure theoreticians that Steklov, for instance, makes them out to be. On the contrary, as soon as Marx had come to the view that any necessary and radical change in the existing social order had to be wholly dependent upon the working class—the proletariat—which in the very conditions of its life was finding all the stimuli, all the impulses that were forcing it into opposition to this system—as soon as Marx was convinced of this, he forthwith went into the midst of the workers; he and Engels tried to penetrate all places, all organisations, where the workers had already been subjected to other influences. Such organisations were already then in existence.

In the account of the history of the workers' movement we have reached the early forties. The League of the Just after the débâcle of May, 1839, ceased to exist as a central organisation.* At any rate, no traces of its existence or its activity as a central organisation are found after 1840. There remained only independent circles organised by ex-members of the League. One of these circles was organised in London.

Other members of the League of the Just fled to Switzerland, the most influential among them being Wilhelm Weitling (1809-1864). A tailor by trade, one of the first German revolutionists from among the artisan proletariat, Weitling, like many other German artisans of the time, peregrinated from town to town. In 1835 he found himself in Paris, but it was in 1837 that he settled there for long. In Paris he became a member of the League of the Just and familiarized himself with the teachings of Hugues Lamennais, the protagonist of Christian socialism, of Saint-Simon and Fourier. There he also met Blanqui and his followers.* Towards the end of 1838 he wrote, at the request of his comrades, a pamphlet called *Mankind As It Is and As It Ought To Be*, in which he championed the ideas of communism.

In Switzerland Weitling and some friends, after an unsuccessful attempt to propagandise the Swiss, began to organise circles among the German workers and the emigrants. In 1842 he published his chief work, *Guarantees of Harmony and Freedom*. In this book he developed in greater detail the views he had expressed in 1838.

Influenced by Blanqui, Weitling's ideas differed from those of other contemporary utopians, in that he did not believe in a peaceful transition into communism. The new society, a very detailed plan of which was worked out by him, could only be realised through the use of force. The sooner existing society is abolished, the sooner will the people be freed. The best method is to bring the existing social disorder to the last extreme. The worse, the better! The most trustworthy revolutionary element which could be relied upon to wreck present society was, according to Weitling, the lowest grade proletariat, the *lumpenproletariat,* including even the robbers.

It was in Switzerland, too, that Michael Bakunin (1814-1876) met Weitling and absorbed some of his ideas. Owing to the arrest and the judicial prosecution started against Weitling and his followers, Bakunin was compromised and forever became an exile from his own country.

After a term in prison, Weitling was extradited to Germany in 1844. Following a period of wandering, he finally landed in London where his arrival was joyously celebrated.

A large mass meeting was arranged in his honour. English socialists and Chartists as well as German and French emigrants participated. This was the first great international meeting in London. It suggested to Schapper the idea of organising, in October, 1844, an international society, The Society of Democratic Friends of all Nations. The aim was the rapprochement of the revolutionists of all nationalities, the strengthening of a feeling of brotherhood among peoples, and the conquest of social and political rights. At the head of this enterprise were Schapper and his friends.

Weitling stayed in London for about a year and a half. In the labour circles, where all kinds of topics dealing with current events were being passionately discussed, Weitling had at first exerted a great influence. But he soon came upon strong opposition. His old comrades, Schapper, Heinrich Bauer and Joseph Moll (1811-1849), had during their much longer stay in London, learned all about the English labour movement and the teachings of Owen.

According to Weitling the proletariat was not a separate class with distinct class interests; the proletariat was only a portion of the indigent oppressed section of the population. Among these poor, the *lumpenproletariat* was the most revolutionary element. He was still trumpeting his idea that robbers and bandits were the most reliable elements in the war against the existing order. He did not attach much weight to propaganda. He visualised the future in the form of a communist society directed by a small group of wise men. To attract the masses, he deemed it indispensable to resort to the aid of religion. He made Christ the forerunner of communism, picturing communism as Christianity minus its later accretions.

To better understand the friction that subsequently developed between him and Marx and Engels, it is well to remember that Weitling was a very able worker, self-taught and gifted with a literary talent, but handicapped by all the limitations of those who are self-educated.

The tendency of an autodidact is to try to get out of his own head something extra-new, to invent some intricate device. He is often doomed to find himself in a foolish predicament, as after a great expenditure of labour he discovers a long-discovered America.

An autodidact may be in search of a *perpetuum mobile;* he may invent a funnel of wisdom whereby one might become a savant before one counts two. Weitling belonged to this class of autodidacts. He wanted to contrive a system of teaching that would enable man to master all sciences in a very short time. He wanted to devise a universal language. It is characteristic that another worker-autodidact, Pierre Proudhon (1809-1865), also laboured over a solution of this problem. As to Weitling, it was at times difficult to determine what he preferred, what was dearer to him—communism, or a universal language. A veritable prophet, he brooked no criticism. He nursed a particular distrust for people learned in books who used to regard his hobby with scepticism.

In 1844 Weitling was one of the most popular and renowned men, not only among German workers but also among the German intelligentsia. We have a characteristic description of a meeting between the famous tailor and the famous poet Heine. Heine writes:

"What particularly offended my pride was the fellow's utter lack of respect while he conversed with me. He did not remove his cap and, while I was standing before him, he remained sitting with his right knee raised to his very chin, with the aid of his right hand, and steadily rubbing with his left hand the raised leg, just above the ankle. At first, I thought this disrespectful attitude to be the result of a habit he had acquired while working at the tailoring trade, but I was soon convinced of my error. When I asked him why he was continually rubbing his leg in this manner, Weitling responded in a nonchalant manner, as if it were the most ordinary occurrence, that in the various German prisons in which he had been confined, he had been kept in chains; and as the iron ring which held his knee was frequently too small, he had developed a chronic irritation of the skin which was the cause for the perpetual scratching of his leg. I confess, I recoiled when the tailor Weitling told me of these chains."

(Yet the poet had suggested the contradictory nature of the feelings which animate the human breast): "I, who had once in Münster kissed with burning lips the relics of the tailor John of Leyden—the chains he had worn, the tongs with which he was tormented, and which have been preserved at the Münster City Hall, I, who had made an exalted cult of the dead tailor, now felt an insurmountable aversion for this living tailor, Wilhelm Weitling, though both were apostles and martyrs in the same cause."

Though Heine discloses himself in not a particularly favourable light, we can nevertheless see that Weitling made a strong impression upon the universally admired poet. The revolutionist could easily distinguish in Heine the intellectual and artistic aristocrat who beholds with curiosity though not without aversion the type of a revolutionary fighter who is strange to him. Marx's attitude to Weitling was quite different, though Marx, too, was an intellectual. To him Weitling was a very gifted expression of the aspirations of that very proletariat, the historic mission of which he himself was then formulating. Here is what he wrote of Weitling before he met him:

"Where can the bourgeoisie, its philosophers and literati included, boast of work dealing with the political emancipation, comparable with Weitling's *Guarantees of Harmony and Freedom?* If one compares the dry and timid mediocrity of German political literature with this fiery and brilliant début of the German workers, if one compares these halting but gigantic first steps of the proletariat with the mincing gait of the full-grown German bourgeoisie, one cannot help predicting that the proletarian Cinderella will develop into a prodigy of strength."

It was quite natural that Marx and Engels should seek to make the acquaintance of Weitling. We know that the two friends during their short sojourn in London in 1845, became acquainted with the English Chartists and with the German emigrants. Though Weitling was still in London at that time, we are not certain that Marx and Engels met him. They entered into close relations in 1846, when Weitling came to Brussels where Marx, too, had settled in 1845 after he had been driven out of France.

By that time Marx was completely engrossed in organisational work. Brussels was very convenient for this purpose, for it was a transit station between France and Germany. German workers and German intellectuals wending their way to Paris invariably stopped for a few days in Brussels. It was from Brussels that forbidden literature was smuggled into, and disseminated all over, Germany. Among the workers who had temporarily settled in Brussels there were few very able men.

Marx soon advanced the idea of convoking a congress of all the communists for the purpose of creating the first all-communist organisation. The Belgian city Verviers near the German border, and therefore convenient for the German communists, was chosen as the place of the meeting. We are not certain whether this convention ever took place, but according to Engels, all the preparations for it had been thought out by Marx long before the delegates from the League of the Just arrived from London with an invitation for the two friends to join the League.

It is obvious why Marx and Engels should have considered the circles which were under the sway of Weitling as being of supreme importance. They had wasted a good deal of effort to meet him on a common platform, but the whole affair culminated in a break. The history of this break was recorded by the Russian critic, Annenkov, who happened to be in Brussels during the Spring of 1846. He left us a very curious description containing an abundance of misrepresentation including, however, a bit of truth. He gives us a report of one meeting at which a furious quarrel occurred between Marx and Weitling. We learn that Marx, pounding his fist on the table, shouted at Weitling, "Ignorance never helped nor did anybody any good." This is quite conceivable, particularly since Weitling, like Bakunin, was opposed to propagandistic and preparatory work. They maintained that paupers were always ready to revolt, that a revolution, therefore, could be engineered at any moment provided there be resolute leaders on hand.

From a letter written by Weitling concerning this meeting, we learn that Marx pressed the following points: a thorough cleansing in the ranks of the communists; a criticism of the useless theoreticians; a renunciation of any socialism that was based on mere good-will; the realisation that communism will be preceded by an epoch during which the bourgeoisie will be at the helm.

In May, 1846, the final rupture came. Weitling soon left for America where he remained until the Revolution of 1848.

Marx and Engels, aided by some friends, continued the task of organisation. In Brussels they built up the Workers' Educational Society where Marx lectured to the members on Political Economy. Besides the intellectuals such as Wilhelm Wolff (1809-1864) to whom Marx later dedicated the first volume of *Capital*, they had as their associates a number of workers like Stefan Born (1824-1899) and others.

With this organisation as a basis, and using their comrades who were travelling between Brussels and other points, Marx and Engels strove to form and to consolidate connections with circles that existed in Germany, London, Paris and Switzerland. Engels himself fulfilled this task in Paris. Gradually the number of those who inclined to the new views of Marx and Engels increased. Then, in order to unite all the communist elements, Marx decided upon the following plan: Instead of a national, purely German organisation, Marx now dreamed of an international one. To begin with, it was imperative to create groups, nuclei of the more mature communists in Brussels, Paris and London. These groups were to choose committees for the purpose of maintaining communication with other communist organisations. Thus was laid the foundation of the future international association. At the suggestion of Marx these committees were styled the Communist Committees for Interrelation (Correspondence Committees).

Since the history of German socialism and the labour movement was written by literateurs and journalists who often had occasion to write articles for the press, or to be members of correspondence or press bureaus, they concluded that the "Correspondence Committees" were nothing else than ordinary correspondence bureaus. It appeared to them that Marx and Engels established a correspondence bureau in Brussels from which they sent out printed circulars and correspondence. Or, as Mehring wrote in his work on Marx:

"Not having had their own organ, Marx and his friends strove to fill the gap as much as was possible by resorting to printed or multigraphed circular letters. At the same time they endeavoured to secure themselves with permanent correspondents from those large centres where communists lived. Such correspondence bureaus existed in Brussels and London. A similar bureau was to be established in Paris. Marx wrote to Proudhon asking for his co-operation."

Yet it is sufficient to read Proudhon's reply a bit more attentively to see that he talks of something wholly different from the usual correspondence bureau. And if we recall that this letter to Marx belongs to the summer of 1846, then we must conclude that long before Marx received the invitation from the London delegation to enter the already defunct League of the Just, there existed in London, in Brussels and in Paris, organisations the initiative for which emanated no doubt from Marx.

Thus toward the second half of 1846 there was a well-organised central correspondence committee in Brussels where all the reports were sent. It was made up of a considerable number of members, some of whom were workers. There was also the Paris committee, organised by Engels and carrying on very active work among the German artisans. Then there was the London committee headed by Schapper, Bauer, and that same Moll who half a year later came to Brussels presumably to urge Marx to become a member of the League of the Just. But as is shown in a letter dated January 20, 1847, this Moll came representing not the League of the Just, but the Communist Correspondence Committee, and he came personally to report on the state of affairs in the London society.

We must conclude then that the story, about the forming of the Communist League, which was started by Engels and which still travels from book to book, is nothing but a legend.

Marx's organisation work has been almost completely overlooked by the investigators; he has been transformed into a cloistered thinker. One of the most interesting sides of his personality has been neglected. Were we to fail to realise the important rôle which Marx—and not Engels— played during the second half of the forties as the director and inspirer of all the preparatory work, we would not understand the tremendous part he subsequently performed as organiser in 1848-49 and during the period of the First International.

After Moll's visit to Brussels, probably, when Marx became convinced that most of the Londoners had freed themselves from Weitling's influence, the convocation of a congress at London was decided upon on the initiative of the Brussels committee. Pre-convention discussions and conflicts between various tendencies began. It was worst of all in Paris, where Engels worked. When one reads his letters, one is convinced that Engels was a capable politician. It appeared, for instance, to Engels that he won a victory, of which he solemnly informs the Brussels committee, not only because he succeeded in persuading the vacillating ones but also because he "put it over" on some, and "bamboozled" others.

In the summer of 1847 the congress convened in London. Marx was not present. Wilhelm Wolff represented Brussels and Engels the Parisian communists.* There were only a few delegates, but this perturbed no one. They decided to unite in the Communist League. This was not a reorganisation of the old League of the Just as Engels, who apparently forgot that he represented the Paris communist committee which he had himself founded, assures us. A constitution was adopted, the first paragraph of which clearly and definitely formulated the basic idea of revolutionary communism.

"The aim of the League is the overthrow of the bourgeoisie, the rule of the proletariat, the abolition of the old bourgeois society based on class antagonisms, and the establishment of a new society without either classes or private property."

The constitution was adopted provisionally. It had to be submitted to the separate committees for discussion and finally adopted at the next convention.

The principle of "democratic centralism" was made the basis of the organisation. It was incumbent upon the members to avow the communist creed, to live in accordance with the aims of the League. A definite group of members formed the basic unit of organisation—the nucleus. This was called a commune. These were combined into districts with their district committees. The various districts were united under the control of a special leading district. The leading districts were responsible to the central committee.

This organisation subsequently became the pattern for all communist working-class parties in their first stages of development. It, however, had one peculiarity which vanished later, but which was still to be met with in Germany up to the beginning of the seventies. The central committee of the Communist League was not elected by the convention. Its powers, as the chief leading centre, were delegated to the district committee of any city designated by the convention as the seat of the central committee. If London was designated, then the organisation of the London district elected a central committee of at least five members. This secured for it close contact with a vast national organisation.

It was also decided by the convention to work out a project for a communist "catechism of faith" which should become the programme of the League. Each district was to offer its own project at the next convention. It was further resolved that a popular journal was to be published. It was the first working-class organ that frankly called itself "communist." It was published half a year before the *Communist Manifesto*, but it already had as its slogan "Workers of all countries, unite!"*

The publication of this journal never went beyond the trial number. The articles were written and printed mainly by members of the Communist League who lived in London. The leading article was in a very popular style. In simple language it pointed out the peculiarities of the new communist organisation and wherein it differed from Weitling's and from the French organisations. There was no mention of the League of the Just. A special article was devoted to the French communist, Etienne Cabet (1788-1856), the author of the famous utopia, *Icaria*. In 1847 Cabet started a lively agitation with the purpose of gathering people who would be willing to migrate to America and to build on its virgin soil, a communist colony along the lines described by him in his *Icaria.*. He even made a special trip to London in the hope of attracting the communists there to his side. The article subjected this plan to a very thorough criticism; it urged the workers not to abandon Europe, for it was there that communism would first be established. There was another long article which had apparently been written by Engels.* In conclusion there was a general social and political survey written undoubtedly by the delegate from Brussels, Wilhelm Wolff.

At the end of 1847, a second congress convened in London. This time Marx was present. Even before he was ready to go to London, Engels had written to him from Paris that he had jotted down an outline of a communist catechism, but that he thought it more advisable to call it *Communist Manifesto*. Marx probably brought to the convention his fully worked-out propositions. Not everything went so smoothly as is described by Steklov. There were violent disagreements. The debates lasted for days and it cost Marx a good deal of labour to convince the majority of the correctness of the new programme. The programme was adopted and the convention charged Marx—and this is important—with writing a manifesto in the name of the League. True, Marx in composing the manifesto availed himself of the project that had been prepared by Engels. But Marx was the only one politically responsible to the League. And if the *Manifesto* makes the impression of a stately monument cast out of one whole block of steel it is completely due to the fact that

Marx alone wrote it. Certainly, many thoughts developed in common by Marx and Engels entered into it, but its cardinal idea, as Engels himself insisted in the following lines, belonged exclusively to Marx:

"The basic ideas of the *Manifesto:* that in every historical epoch, the prevailing mode of production and the social organisation necessarily following from it, form the basis upon which is built the political and intellectual history of that epoch; that consequently at the different stages of social development (since the dissolution of the primitive community of property in the soil) the history of mankind has been a history of class struggles, struggle between exploited and exploiters, oppressed and ruling classes; that this struggle has however now reached a stage where the exploited and oppressed class—the proletariat—cannot attain its emancipation from the exploiting and oppressing class—the bourgeoisie—without, at the same time, and for all time, emancipating society as a whole from all exploitation, oppression, and class struggles—these fundamental ideas belong entirely and solely to Marx."

We should note this circumstance. The Communist League, as well as Engels, knew that the main burden of evolving the new programme fell upon Marx, that it was he who was charged with the writing of the *Manifesto.* We have an interesting letter—interesting in other respects too—substantiating our contention. It casts a curious light on the relations between Marx and the organisation which was proletarian in its spirit and its tendency to regard the "intellectual" as merely an expert at formulating. The better to understand this letter, we must know that London was designated as the seat of the central committee, which was, in accordance with the constitution, selected by the London organisation.

This letter was sent on January 26, 1848, by the central committee to the district committee of Brussels for transmission to Marx. It contains a resolution passed by the central committee on January 24:

"The Central Committee hereby directs the District Committee of Brussels to notify Citizen Marx that if the Manifesto of the Communist Party, which he consented, at the last Congress, to draw up, does not reach London before Tuesday, February 1, further measures will be taken against him. In case Citizen Marx does not write the Manifesto, the Central Committee requests the immediate return of the documents which were turned over to him by the congress.

"In the name and at the instruction of the Central Committee,
(Signed) Schapper, Bauer, Moll."

We see from this angry missive that even toward the end of January, Marx was not through with the work handed over to him in December. This, too, is very typical of Marx. With all his literary ability he was a bit slow of movement. He generally laboured long over his works, particularly if it was an important document. He wanted this document to be invested with the most nearly perfect form, that it might withstand the ravages of time. We have one page from Marx's first draft, it shows how painstakingly Marx laboured over each phrase.

The central committee did not have to resort to any further measures. Marx evidently succeeded in completing his task toward the beginning of February. This is worth noting. The *Manifesto* was issued a few days before the February Revolution. From this we may deduce, of course, that the *Manifesto* could hardly have played any part in the matter of preparing for the February Revolution. And after we discover that the first copies of the *Manifesto* did not make their way into Germany before May or June of 1848, we can make the further deduction that the German Revolution, too, was not much affected by this document. Its contents were known only to a small group of Brussels and London communists.

The *Manifesto* was the programme of the international Communist League. This League was composed of a few Belgians, some communist-minded English Chartists, and most of all, of Germans. The *Manifesto* had to take in consideration not any one particular country, but the whole bourgeois world before which the communists for the first time openly expounded their aims.

The first chapter presents a striking and clear picture of bourgeois, capitalist society, of the class struggle which had created it and which continued to develop within this society. We see the inevitable inception of the bourgeoisie in the womb of the old mediæval feudal system. We watch the changing conditions in the existence of the bourgeoisie in response to the changes in economic relations. We observe the revolutionary rôle it played in its combat with feudalism and to what extraordinary degree it fostered the development of the productive forces of human society, having thus for the first time in history created the possibility of the material liberation of all mankind.

Then follows an historical sketch of the evolution of the proletariat. We see how the proletariat developed as inevitably as the bourgeoisie, and concomitantly with it. We see how it gradually integrated into a separate class. Before us pass the various forms which the conflict between the proletariat and the bourgeoisie assumed before the proletariat became a class for itself, and before it created its own class organisation.

The *Manifesto* further presents and subjects to an annihilating criticism all the objections to communism advanced by the ideologists of the bourgeoisie.

Marx—and here he relied on Engels, though not to the extent that we imagined—further explains the tactics of the communists with respect to other workingmen's parties. Here we encounter an interesting detail. The *Manifesto* declares that the communists do not constitute a separate party in contradistinction to other workingmen's parties. They are merely the vanguard of the workers, and their advantage over the remaining mass of the proletariat is in their understanding of the conditions, direction, and general results of the labour movement.

Now that we know the actual history of the Communist League, it is easier to explain such a statement of the problems of the communists. It was dictated by the state of the labour movement at that time, particularly that of the English movement. Those Chartists who agreed to enter the League did it on condition that they be allowed to maintain their connections with their old party. They only took upon themselves the obligation of organising within Chartism something in the nature of a communist nucleus for the purpose of disseminating there the programme and the ideas of communism.

The *Manifesto* analyses minutely the numerous tendencies that were striving for ascendancy among the socialists and the communists. It subjects them to a most incisive criticism and definitely rejects them, all except the great utopians—Saint Simon, Fourier, and Owen—whose teachings Marx and Engels had to a certain degree adopted and remodelled. Accepting their criticism of the bourgeois order, the *Manifesto* pits against the pacific, utopian, non-political socialism, the revolutionary programme of the new proletarian—critical communism.

In conclusion the *Manifesto* examines the communist tactics at the time of a revolution, particularly with respect to the bourgeois parties. The procedure varies with each country, depending on its specific historical conditions. Where the bourgeoisie is already dominant, the proletariat wages war exclusively against it. In those countries where the bourgeoisie is still striving for political power, as for instance in Germany, the communist party works hand in hand with the bourgeoisie, as long as the latter fights against the monarchy and the nobility.

Yet the communists never cease instilling into the minds of the workers an ever-keener consciousness of the truth that the interests of the bourgeoisie are diametrically opposed to those of the proletariat. The crucial question always remains that of private property. These were the tactical rules worked out by Marx and Engels on the eve of the February and the March Revolutions of 1848. We shall subsequently see how these rules were applied in practice, and how they were changed as a result of revolutionary experience.

We now have a general idea of the contents of the *Manifesto*. We must bear in mind that it incorporated the results of all the scientific work which Engels and particularly Marx had performed from 1845 to the end of 1847. During this period Engels succeeded in getting into shape the material he had collected for his *Condition of the Working Class in England*, and Marx laboured over the history of political and economic thought. During these two years, in the struggle against all kinds of idealist teachings, they pretty adequately developed the materialistic conception of history which enabled them to orient themselves so well in their study of the material relations, the conditions of production and distribution which always determine social relations.

The new teaching had been most completely and clearly expounded by Marx even before the *Manifesto*, in his polemic against Proudhon. In the *Holy Family*, Marx spoke very highly of Proudhon. What was it then that provoked the break between the two old allies?

Proudhon, like Weitling, was a worker and an autodidact. He subsequently became one of the outstanding French publicists. He set out upon his literary career in a very revolutionary spirit. In his book, *What Is Property?* which was published in 1841, he criticised most acutely the institution of private property, and he came to the daring conclusion that in its essence private property is robbery. In reality, however, Proudhon condemned only one form of property, the capitalistic, which was based upon the exploitation of the small producer by the big capitalist. Having nothing against the abolition of capitalistic private property, Proudhon was at the same time opposed to communism. The only security for the welfare of the peasant and the artisan was according to him the preservation and the enhancement of their private property. The condition of the worker could be improved, in his opinion, not by means of strikes and economic warfare, but by converting the worker into a property-owner. He finally arrived at these views in 1845 and 1846 when he first formulated a plan whereby he thought it possible to insure the artisan against ruin, and to transform the proletarian into an independent producer.

We have already mentioned the rôle that Engels at that time played in Paris. His chief opponent in the discussion of programmes was Karl Grün (1813-1884) who represented "real socialism."* Grün was very intimately allied with Proudhon, whose views he expounded before the German workers living in Paris. Even before Proudhon published his new book in which he wanted to expose all the "economic contradictions" in existing society, and to explain the origin of poverty, the "philosophy of poverty," he communicated his new plan to Grün. The latter hastened to use it in his polemics against the communists. Engels hurried to communicate this plan to the Brussels committee.

"But what was this plan which was to save the world? Nothing more or less than the well-known and bankrupt English Labour Exchanges run by associations of various craftsmen. All that is required is a large depot; all the products delivered by the members of the association are to be evaluated according to the prices of the raw materials plus the labour, and paid for in other products evaluated in precisely the same way. The products in excess of the needs of the association are to be sold in the world market, and the receipts are to be turned over to the producers. Thus, thinks the cunning Proudhon, the profits of the commercial middleman might be eliminated to the advantage of himself and his confederates."

In his letter Engels communicated new details of Proudhon's plan and was indignant that such fantasies as the transformation of workers into property-owners by the purchase of workshops on their savings still attracted the German workers.

Immediately upon the appearance of Proudhon's *Philosophy of Poverty*, Marx sat down to work and wrote in 1847 his little book, *Poverty of Philosophy*, in which, step by step, he overthrew the ideas of Proudhon. But he did not confine himself merely to destructive criticism; he expounded his own fully developed ideas of communism. By its brilliance and keenness of thought and by its correctness of statement this book was a worthy introduction to the *Communist Manifesto*, and was not inferior to the last comments Marx wrote on Proudhon in 1874 in an article on "Political Indifference." This proves that Marx had developed his fundamental points of view by 1847.

Marx vaguely formulated his ideas for the first time in 1845. Two more years of assiduous work were required for Marx to be able to write his *Poverty of Philosophy*. While studying the circumstances under which the proletariat was formed and had developed in bourgeois society, he delved deeper and deeper into the laws of production and distribution under the capitalist system. He re-examined the teachings of bourgeois economists in the light of the dialectic method and he showed that the fundamental categories, the phenomena of bourgeois society—commodity, value, money, capital—represent something transitory. In his *Poverty of Philosophy*, he made the first attempt to indicate the important phases in the development of the process of capitalist production. This was only the first draft, but from this it was already obvious that Marx was on the right track, that he had a true method, a splendid compass, by the aid of which he confidently made his way through the thickets of bourgeois economy. But this book also proved that it was not sufficient to be in possession of a correct method, that one could not limit himself to general conclusions, that it was necessary to make a careful study of capitalist reality, in order that one might penetrate into all the subtleties of this intricate mechanism. Marx had a colossal task before him; this first draft, though the work of a genius, still had to be converted into a stately edifice. But before Marx had a chance to build this edifice, he and Engels had to go through the Revolution of 1848, which they had been impatiently awaiting, which they had foretold, for which they had been preparing, and in anticipation of which they had worked out the basic propositions of the *Communist Manifesto*.

CHAPTER V

THE *Communist Manifesto* was published only a few days before the February Revolution, and the organisation of the Communist League was brought to completion only in November, 1847. The League which was composed of the Paris, London and Brussels circles, was only loosely connected with some smaller German groups.

This in itself is sufficient to show that the organised forces of the German sections of the Communist League with which Marx had to operate were quite insignificant. The Revolution flared up in Paris on February 24, 1848. It spread rapidly to Germany. On March 3 there was something of a popular insurrection in Cologne, the chief city in the Rhine province. The city authorities were forced to address a petition to the Prussian King; they implored him to heed this disturbance and to make some concessions. At the head of this Cologne insurrection there were two men, Gotschalk, a physician who was very popular among the poor and the workers of Cologne, and the ex-officer, August Willich (1810-1878). On March 13, the Revolution broke out in Vienna, on the 18th it reached Berlin.

During all this time Marx was in Brussels. The Belgian government, not wishing to share the fate of the July monarchy swooped down upon the immigrants who resided in Brussels, arrested Marx, and within a few hours conducted him out of the country. He went to Paris. One of the heads of the provisional government of France, Ferdinand Flocon (1800-1866), an editor of a newspaper to which Engels was a contributor, had previously invited Marx to come, declaring that on the now free French soil all the decrees of the old government were null and void.

The Brussels district committee, to whom the London committee had handed over its authority after the revolutionary outbreaks on the continent, transferred its authority to Marx. Among the German workers who congregated in Paris in large numbers, many dissensions arose and various groups were organised. One of these groups was under the sway of Bakunin who, together with the German poet Georg Herwegh (1817-1875), hatched a plan of forming an armed organisation and invading Germany.

Marx tried to dissuade them from this enterprise; he suggested that they go to Germany singly, and participate in the revolutionary events there. But Bakunin and Herwegh adhered to their old plan. Herwegh organised a revolutionary legion, and led it to the German border, where he was completely defeated. Marx together with some comrades succeeded in getting into Germany, where they settled in different places. Marx and Engels went to the Rhine province.

We must remember that the German section of the Communist League had no organisation. There were only isolated sympathisers. What was there left for Marx, Engels and their comrades to do? About forty years after the events described here, Engels tried to explain to the young comrades the tactics which he and Marx had pursued in Germany in 1848. To a question, "why did he and Marx stay in the Rhine province, in Cologne, instead of going to Berlin?" he gave the following clear answer: They chose the Rhine province because industrially it was the most developed part of Germany; because it was under the system of the Napoleonic code—a heritage of the French Revolution, and they could, therefore, expect greater freedom of action, greater latitude for agitation and propaganda. Besides, the Rhine province had an appreciable proletarian element. True, Cologne itself was not among the most industrialised localities in the Rhine province, but in the administrative and every other sense, it was the centre of the province. Considering the times, its population was considerable—eighty thousand inhabitants. Its most important machine industry was sugar refining. The eau-de-Cologne industry, while important, did not require much machinery. The textile industries distinctly lagged behind those of Elberfeld and Barmen. At any rate, Marx and Engels had good reasons for having chosen Cologne as their residence. They wished to keep in touch with the whole of Germany; they wished to found a strong journal which would serve as a tribune for the entire country, and for this, in their opinion, Cologne was the most appropriate place. Was it not in the same province that the first important political organ of the German bourgeoisie had been published in 1842? All the preliminary work for the publication of such an organ had been going on for some time. Marx and Engels succeeded in gaining control of the publication that was being organised.

But this publication was the organ of the democratic groups. Here is how Engels tried to explain why they referred to it as the Organ of Democracy. There had been no proletarian organisation, and there were only two roads they could follow—either the immediate organisation of a communist party, or the utilisation of the democratic organisations that were on hand, first by uniting them all, and then by boring from within, by criticism and propaganda, to effect a reorganisation and to attract workingmen's circles that had not belonged to the democratic organisations before. The second method was chosen. This placed Marx and Engels in a somewhat false position in relation to the Workingmen's Union of Cologne which had been organised by Gotschalk and Willich immediately after the third of March.

Gotschalk was a physician, very popular with the Cologne poor. He was not a communist; in his views he rather approached Weitling and the Weitlingites. He was a good revolutionist, but too easily swayed by moods. Personally he was a man beyond reproach. Though not guided by a definite programme, he was sufficiently critical of democracy to have declared at his first public appearance at the town hall, "I come not in the name of the people, for all these representatives are of the people; no, I address myself to you only in the name of the labouring population." He differentiated between the working class and the people as a whole. He insisted on revolutionary measures, but being a republican he demanded a federation of all the German republics. This was one of the essential points of disagreement between him and Marx. The society founded by him in Cologne, the Workingmen's Union of Cologne, soon embraced almost all the proletarian elements of the city. It counted about seven thousand members. For a city with a population of eighty thousand this was an imposing number.

The Workingmen's Society led by Gotschalk soon entered into a conflict with the organisation to which Marx and Engels belonged. We should note, however, that there were elements within this vast workingmen's organisation that differed with Gotschalk. Moll and Schapper, for instance, though members of the Workingmen's Union, were closely connected with Marx and Engels. Thus within the Union there were soon formed two factions. But the fact remains that alongside the Workingmen's Union of Cologne, there existed a democratic society which counted Marx, Engels and others among its members.

All this resulted from Marx's plan. Everything con-
verged to one point. Marx and Engels had hoped to make
the central organ, which was first published on June 1,
1848, the axis around which all the future communist organisations which would be formed in the process of revolutionary
conflict, would assemble. We must not think that Marx
and Engels entered this democratic organ as democrats.
They did not; they entered as communists who regarded
themselves as the most extreme left wing of the entire democratic organisation. Not for a moment did they cease
vehemently to denounce the errors not only of the German
liberal party, but above all, the errors of the democrats.
They did it so well that they lost their shareholders within
the first few months. In his very first editorial, Marx attacked the democrats most severely. And when the news of
the June defeat of the Paris proletariat arrived, when Cava-
gniac, supported by all the bourgeois parties, swept down
upon the workers, effected a massacre in which several thousands of Paris workers perished, the democratic organ, the
Neue Rheinische Zeitung, published an article which till now
remains unexcelled in power and passion with which it lashes
the bourgeois hangmen and their democratic apologists.

"The workers of Paris were crushed by the superior forces
of their enemies—they were annihilated. They are beaten, but
their enemies are defeated. The momentary triumph of brute
force is purchased with the destruction of all the seductions and
illusions of the February Revolution, with the complete disinte-
gration of the old Republican Party, with the splitting of the
French nation into two parts—a nation of owners, and a nation
of workers. The Republic of the tricolour will henceforth be
of one hue only—the colour of the vanquished, the colour of
blood. It has become a Red Republic.
"The February Revolution was splendid. It was a revolution
of universal sympathies, for the contradictions which flared up
within it against the royal power as yet lay in latent harmony,
slumbering undeveloped side by side, since the social conflict

which was their background had attained merely a phantom existence, the existence of a phrase, a word. The June Revolution, on the contrary, is disgusting, repulsive, for instead of the word emerged the deed, because the Republic itself bared the head of the monster, having dashed from it its protecting and concealing crown.

"Are we democrats to be misled by the deep abyss that gapes before us? Are we to conclude that the struggle for new forms of the State is devoid of meaning, is illusory—a phantasm?

"Only weak, timid minds would ask this question. The conflicts arising from the very conditions of bourgeois society, have to be fought to the end; they cannot be reasoned away. The best form of state is one in which the social contradictions are not overcome by force, in other words, only by artificial and specious means. The best form of state is one in which the contradictions collide in open struggle and thus attain a solution.

"We shall be asked, is it possible that we shall reserve not a single tear, not a sigh, not a word, for the victims of popular frenzy, for the National Guards, for the *guardes mobiles,* for the Republican Guards, for the soldiers of the line?

"The State will take care of their widows and orphans, decrees will glorify them, solemn funeral processions will place their remains in their last resting places, the official press will proclaim them immortal, the European reaction will do homage to them from East to West.

"But the plebeians, ravished by hunger, spat upon by the press, deserted by the physicians, denounced by respectable thieves as incendiaries and jailbirds; their wives and children hurled into still more fathomless poverty, their best representatives, who have survived the slaughter, deported to foreign parts —to crown their menacing and gloomy brows with laurel—this is the privilege, the right and duty, of the democratic press."

This article was written on June 28, 1848. Such an article could not have been written by a democrat; only a communist could have written it. Marx and Engels deceived no one with their tactics. The paper ceased to receive financial support from the democratic bourgeoisie. It had in reality become the organ of the Cologne workers and of the German workers. Other members of the Communist

League, spread all over Germany, continued their work. One of them, Stefan Born, a compositor, is worth mentioning. Engels does not speak favourably of him; Born adopted different tactics. Having found himself from the very beginning in Berlin, in the proletarian centre, he put before himself, as his objective, the creation of a large workingmen's organisation. With the aid of some comrades he established a small journal, *The Brotherhood of Workers*, and conducted a systematic agitation among various types of workers. Unlike Gotschalk and Willich, he did not confine himself merely to organising a workers' political party. Born undertook to organise craft unions and other societies which were to protect the economic interests of the workers. He forged ahead so energetically that he soon attempted to carry over this organisation into a number of neighbouring cities, and to spread it into other parts of Germany. There was one flaw in this organisation—it emphasised the purely economic demands of the workers to the exclusion of other demands. Thus, while some members of the Communist League were forming purely workingmen's organisations all over Germany, in the South there were others who, headed by Marx, used all their strength to reorganise the democratic elements, and to make the working class into a nucleus of an even more democratic party. It was in this spirit that Marx carried on his work.

The *Neue Rheinische Zeitung* reacted upon all fundamental questions. We must admit that up to the present the paper remains the unattainable ideal of revolutionary journalism. Its acuteness of analysis, its freshness, its revolutionary ardour, its breadth and profundity have never been parallelled.

Before we pass over to the discussion of the basic principles upon which the internal and the external policies of the paper were determined, we should examine the revolutionary experience of its editors-in-chief. Neither Marx nor Engels had had any other experience except that which had been provided by the Great French Revolution. Marx had studied most attentively the history of that revolution and had endeavoured to work out principles of tactics for the epoch of the coming revolution which he, contrary to Proudhon, had correctly foreseen. What then did Marx learn from the experience of the French Revolution? The Revolution broke out in 1789. It represented a rather lengthy process; it lasted from 1789 to 1799, that is, up to the year in which Napoleon accomplished his *coup d'état*. The English Revolution of the seventeenth century also suggested that the coming revolution would be a prolonged one. The French Revolution began with universal joy, with universal jubilation. At the very beginning the bourgeoisie assumed the leadership of the oppressed populace, and abolished absolutism. Only later there developed friction within this triumphant bourgeoisie. In the process of this struggle, power was passing to more extreme elements. This struggle lasted for three years, with the result that power had passed into the hands of the Jacobins. To Marx, who had carefully studied the evolution of the Jacobin party, it seemed that in the next revolution, too, it would be possible to direct the forces which would develop spontaneously in the heat of prolonged political action.

This premise explains his error. For long he held to this opinion, and a whole series of events were needed to make him renounce this premise. The first blow the Revolution had received in the West was the June defeat of the Paris proletariat. It immediately gave reaction a chance to raise its head in Prussia, in Austria and in Russia. Nicholas I offered help to the Prussian King from the very start; the armed assistance was rejected but Russian money was cheerfully accepted. It proved exceedingly helpful. To the Austrian Emperor, against whom Hungary had rebelled, Nicholas offered battalions. They were accepted.

The *Neue Rheinische Zeitung*, relying upon the experience of the French Revolution, advocated the following tactics: War with Russia, it seemed, was the only means of saving the Revolution in western Europe. The defeat of the Paris proletariat was the first blow at the Revolution. The history of the Great French Revolution showed that it had been the attack of the Coalition upon France that supplied the impulse for the strengthening of the revolutionary movement. The moderate parties had been thrown aside. The leadership had been taken over by those parties which were able to repel most energetically the external attack. As a result of the attack by the Coalition, France had been declared a republic on August 10, 1792. Marx and Engels expected that a war of the reactionaries against the new Revolution would lead to similar results. That is why they kept on criticising Russia in the columns of their paper. Russia was constantly being pointed out as the power behind Austrian and German reaction. Each editorial tried to prove that war with Russia was the sole means of saving the Revolution. The democratic elements were being prepared for this war as for the only way out. Marx and Engels maintained that war with Russia would give the needed jolt to awaken all the revolutionary passions of the German people. Guided by this view, Marx and Engels defended every oppositional, every revolutionary tendency against the established order. They were the most fervent defenders of the Hungarian Revolution; they most passionately defended the Poles who shortly before had made a fresh attempt at insurrection. They demanded the re-establishment of an independent and united Poland. In the same spirit, they demanded the unification of Germany into one republic, and the restoration to Germany of some districts that had once belonged to Germany, and that were populated with Germans. In short, everywhere did they remain true to the basic principles of the *Communist Manifesto* by supporting every revolutionary movement directed against the established order.

Nevertheless, it should not be overlooked that the articles in the *Neue Rheinische Zeitung* dealt overwhelmingly with the political aspect of things. They were always criticisms of the political acts of the bourgeoisie, or the political acts of the bureaucracy. When we peruse the *Neue Rheinische Zeitung* we are struck by the inadequacy of space allotted to proletarian questions. This was particularly so during the year 1848. Stefan Born's organ, on the contrary, resembled a modern trade-union paper. It was replete with discussions of proletarian affairs. In Marx's paper questions dealing directly with the demands of the working class were very rare. It was almost completely devoted to the excitation of political passions, and to the agitation in favour of the creation of such democratic revolutionary forces which would with one blow free Germany of all the remnants of the obsolete feudal system.

But towards the end of 1848 conditions changed. The reaction which had already begun to gain strength after the June defeat of the Paris proletariat, became even more aggressive in October, 1848. The failure at Vienna served as the signal, and brought in its train the defeat at Berlin. With renewed arrogance the Prussian government dispersed the national assembly and imposed a constitution of its own making. And the Prussian bourgeoisie, in lieu of offering actual resistance, was worrying about establishing harmony between the people and the King's government.

Marx, on the other hand, maintained that the royal power of Prussia suffered defeat in March, 1848, and that there could be no question of an agreement with the crown. The people should adopt its own constitution and, without heeding the royal power, it should declare the country one indivisible German Republic. But the national assembly, in which there was a preponderance of the liberal and democratic bourgeoisie, fearsome of a final break with the monarchy, kept on preaching compromise until it was dispersed.

Finally Marx was persuaded that no hope could be placed even on the most extreme faction of the German bourgeoisie. Even the democratic faction of the middle class which could be expected to create free political conditions conducive to the development of the working class proved its utter ineptitude for the task.

Here is how Marx, on the basis of the sad experiences of the Berlin and Frankfort assemblies, characterised the bourgeoisie in December, 1848:

"While the Revolutions of 1648 and 1789 had been inspired with a boundless feeling of pride, standing, as they did, on the threshold of a new era, the pride of the Berliners in 1848 was based on the fact that they represented an anachronism. Their light was not unlike the light of those stars whose rays reach the denizens of our earth 100,000 years after the extinction of the luminary which sent them forth. The Prussian Revolution of March represented in miniature—it represented nothing except in miniature—such a star in Europe. Its light was the light of a social corpse long since decayed.

"The German bourgeoisie had developed so languidly, so timidly, so slowly, that when it began to constitute a danger to feudalism and absolutism, it already found itself opposed on the other hand by the proletariat and all those strata of the city population the interests and ideas of which were identical with those of the proletariat. Its enemy included not only the class *behind* it but all of Europe *in front*. As distinguished from the French bourgeoisie of 1789, the Prussian bourgeoisie was not the class that would defend the whole of contemporary society against the representatives of the old order, the monarchy, the nobility. It had declined to the level of an estate which was in opposition to the crown as well as to the people, and was irresolute in its relations to either of its enemies because it was always beholding both of them either before it or behind its back; it was inclined from the very start to betray the people and to make compromises with the crowned representative of the old society, for the German bourgeoisie itself belonged to the old

society; it represented the interests not of a new order against
the old, but interests within the old order, which have taken on
a new lease of life; it stood at the helm of the revolution not because it was backed by the people, but because the people had
shoved it to the front; it found itself at the head not because it
took the initiative in favour of the new social epoch, but merely
because it represented the discontent of the obsolete social
epoch; it was a stratum of the old State which had not yet
effected its emergence, but which was now flung to the surface
of the new State by an upheaval; without faith in itself, without
faith in the people, grumbling against the upper class, trembling
before the lower classes, selfish in its attitude toward both, and
aware of its selfishness, revolutionary with respect to the conservatives, and conservative with respect to the revolutionists,
distrustful of its own slogans, which were phrases instead of
ideas, intimidated by the world storm, yet exploiting that very
storm, devoid of energy in any direction, yet resorting to plagia-
rism in all directions, banal through lack of originality, but original in its sheer banality, entering into compromises with its own
desires, without initiative, without faith in itself, without faith
in the people, without a universal historical calling, a doomed
senile creature, devoted to the impossible task of leading and
manipulating the robust youthful aspirations of a new people in
his own senile interests—sans eyes, sans ears, sans teeth, sans
everything—such was the position of the Prussian bourgeoisie
that had been guiding the destinies of the Prussian State since
the March Revolution."

The hope which Marx had placed in the progressive bourgeoisie, in the *Manifesto*, although even there he enumerated
a series of conditions precedent to real co-operation with it,
was not justified. Towards the Fall of 1848, Marx and
Engels changed their tactics. Not rejecting the support of
the bourgeois democrats, nor severing his relations with the
democratic organisation, Marx, nevertheless, shifted the
centre of his activity into the proletarian midst. Together
with Moll and Schapper, he concentrated his work in the
Workingmen's Union of Cologne which, too, had its representative in the District Committee of Democratic Societies.

The fact that upon Gotschalk's arrest, Moll was elected chairman of the Workingmen's Union indicates the increased strength of the communists.   The federalist trend which was headed by Gotschalk gradually faded into a minority. When Moll was forced for a time to flee Cologne, Marx, despite the fact that he had repeatedly declined the honour, was elected chairman in his stead.   In February, during the elections for the new parliament, disagreements arose. Marx and his followers insisted that the workers, where there was no chance of electing their own representatives, should vote for democrats.   The minority protested against this.

In March and April, friction between the workers and the democrats who were united in the District Committee of the Democratic Societies reached a stage where a schism was unavoidable.   Marx and his supporters resigned from the Committee.   The Workingmen's Union recalled its representative and proceeded to ally itself with the workingmen's societies which had been organised by Stefan Born in eastern Germany.   The Workingmen's Union itself was reorganised into the Central Club with nine regional branches, workingmen's clubs.   Towards the end of April, Marx and Schapper issued a proclamation which invited all the workingmen's societies throughout the Rhine province and Westphalia to a regional congress for the purpose of organisation and for the election of deputies to the General Workingmen's Congress which was to take place in June at Leipzig.

But just as Marx and his followers were setting out upon the organisation of a labour party, a new blow was struck at the Revolution.   Having put an end to the Prussian National Assembly, the government decided also to put an end to the German National Assembly.   It was in southern Germany that the fight for the so-called Imperial Constitution began.

We must point out one more detail which is generally overlooked by Marx's biographers.   Marx's position in Cologne was precarious; his behaviour had to be exceedingly circumspect. Though he did not have to live underground, he was, nevertheless, subject to expulsion from Cologne by a mere government order. Here is how it came about that Marx found himself in this unique predicament.

Having been exposed to the incessant persecutions of the Prussian Government, having been expelled from Paris on the insistence of the same government, and having feared deportation from Belgium, Marx finally resolved to renounce his allegiance to Prussia. He did not declare his allegiance to any other country, but definitely renounced his Prussian one. The Prussian government seized upon it. When Marx returned to Cologne, the local authorities recognised him as a citizen of the Rhine province, but they demanded that the Prussian authorities in Berlin confirm it. The latter decided that Marx had lost his rights of citizenship. That is why Marx, who was trying very hard for a reinstatement into the rights of Prussian citizenship, was compelled in the second half of 1848 to desist from making public appearances. When the revolutionary wave would rise and conditions would improve, Marx appeared openly before the public; as soon as the wave of reaction would rise and repressions in Cologne would become more furious, Marx vanished and confined himself only to literary work, that is, to the directing of the *Neue Rheinische Zeitung*. This is why Marx was so reluctant to become chairman of the Workingmen's Union of Cologne.

In accord with the change in tactics, there was a turn in the policy of the *Neue Rheinische Zeitung*. The first articles on *Wage Labour and Capital* appeared only after the change. These were prefaced by a long statement in which Marx explained why the paper had never before touched upon the antagonism between capital and labour. The change, however, was made too late. It took place in February, while in May the German revolution was already completely crushed.

The ferocity of the Prussian government swept like a storm across the country. Its armies swooped down upon the southwest. The *Neue Rheinische Zeitung* was among the first casualties. It was discontinued on May 19, when the famous red number was published. (Besides a beautiful poem by Ferdinand Freiligrath [1810-1876], that issue contained Marx's address to the working class warning them against provocations by the government.) After this, Marx left the Rhine province, and as a foreigner, had to abandon Germany. The rest of the staff left for various places. Engels, Moll, and Willich went to join the south German rebels.

After several weeks of heroic but badly organised resistance against the Prussian armies, the rebels were forced to cross over into Switzerland. The ex-members of the staff of the *Neue Rheinische Zeitung* and of the Workingmen's Union of Cologne peregrinated to Paris, but in 1849, after the unsuccessful demonstration of June 13, they, too, fell under the ban and were forced to leave France. Towards the beginning of 1850 there came together, in London, almost the entire old guard of the Communist League. Moll had perished during the insurrection in the south. Marx, Engels, Schapper, Willich, and Wolff found themselves in London.

Marx and Engels, as may be gleaned from their writings of that period, did not at first lose hope. They felt that this was only a temporary halt in the march of the revolution and that a fresh and greater upheaval was bound to follow. In order that they might not be caught unawares, they wished to strengthen the organisation, and to tie it up more securely with Germany. The old Communist League was reorganised; the old elements as well as the new ones from Silesia, Breslau and the Rhine provinces were drawn in.

Very soon, however, differences began to spring up. The controversy came to a head on the following question:

Even at the beginning of 1850, Marx and Engels thought

that it would not be long ere the revolution would be resuscitated. It was precisely at this time that two famous circulars were released by the Communist League. Lenin, who knew them by heart, used to delight in quoting them.

In these circulars—and they can only be understood if we recall the errors made by Marx and Engels during the Revolution of 1848—we find that besides mercilessly criticising bourgeois liberalism, we must also attack the democratic elements. We must muster all our strength to create a workingmen's party in opposition to the democratic organisation. The democrats must be lashed and flayed. If they demand a ten-hour workday, we should demand an eight-hour day. If they demand expropriation of large estates with just compensation, then we must demand confiscation without compensation. We must use every possible means to goad on the revolution, to make it permanent, and not to let it lapse into desuetude. We cannot afford to be satisfied with the immediate conquests. Each bit of conquered territory must serve as a step for further conquests. Every attempt to declare the revolution consummated is treason to its cause. We must exert our strength, to the last bit, to undermine and destroy the social and political fabric in which we live, until the last vestiges of the old class antagonisms are eradicated forever.

Differences of opinion arose about the evaluation of the existing conditions. In contradistinction to his opponents, the most important among whom were Schapper and Willich, Marx, true to his method, insisted that every political revolution was the effect of definite economic causes, of a certain economic revolution. The Revolution of 1848 was preceded by the economic crisis of 1847 which had held all of Europe, except the Far East, in its grip. Having studied in London the prevailing economic conditions, the state of the world market, Marx came to the conclusion that the new situation was not favourable to a revolutionary eruption, and that the absence of the new revolutionary upheaval, which he and his friends had been anticipating, might be explained otherwise than by the lack of revolutionary initiative and revolutionary energy on the part of the revolutionists. On the basis of his detailed analysis of the existing conditions, he reached the conclusion, at the end of 1850, that in the face of such economic efflorescence any attempt to force a revolution, to induce an uprising, was doomed to fruitless defeat. And conditions were then particularly conducive to the development of European capital. Fabulously rich gold mines were discovered in California and in Australia; vast hosts of workers rushed into these countries. The deluge of European emigration started in 1848 and reached tremendous proportions in 1850.

Thus, a study of economic conditions brought Marx to the conviction that the revolutionary wave was receding and that there would be no renewal of the revolutionary movement until another economic crisis arose and created more favourable conditions. Some of the members of the Communist League did not subscribe to these views. These views met with the particular disapproval of those who were not well grounded in economics and who attached inordinate importance to the revolutionary initiative of a few resolute individuals. Willich, Schapper, a number of other members of the Cologne Workingmen's Union, and the old Weitlingites, coalesced. They insisted upon the necessity of forcing a revolutionary uprising in Germany. All they needed, they claimed, was a certain sum of money, and a number of daring individuals. They began to hunt for money. An effort was made to solicit a loan from America, a loan with a German revolution as its objective. Marx, Engels and a few of their near friends refused to participate in this campaign. Finally a schism occurred, and the Communist League was split into a Marx-Engels faction and a Willich-Schapper faction.

It happened that at this very time one section of the Communist League which was still in Germany, came to grief. It was since 1850 that Marx and Engels were making an effort to strengthen the League in Germany along with its reorganisation in London.   Emissaries were sent to Germany with the purpose of establishing closer ties with the German communists.   One of them was arrested.   The papers that were found on him revealed the names of all his comrades.   A number of communists were jailed.   The Prussian government, in order to demonstrate to the German bourgeoisie that the latter had no reason to regret the few privileges it had lost in 1850, staged an imposing trial of the communists.   The upshot was a few long-term sentences for several communists who included Friedrich Lessner.[1*]   During the trial certain ugly facts came to the surface—the agent provocateur, Stieber, the falsification of minutes, perjury, etc.

At the suggestion of the communists who stood with Marx, he wrote a pamphlet in which he exposed the nefarious work of the Prussian police in connection with the persecution of the communists.   This, however, proved of little assistance to the condemned.   Upon the termination of the trial, Marx, Engels and their comrades came to the conclusion that, in face of this unfortunate turn of events, and since all revolutionary connections with Germany were severed, the League had nothing to do but to wait for a more auspicious time; in 1852 the Communist League was officially disbanded.   The other part of the Communist League, the Willich-Schapper faction, vegetated for another year.   Some left for America.[2]   Schapper remained in London.   A few years later he came to realise the errors he had made in 1852, and again made peace with Marx and Engels.

[1] Dr. Abraham Jacobi who later became a noted physician in New York was one of the defendants at this trial.
[2] Willich fought in the Civil War as a General in the Northern Army.

CHAPTER VI

WITH the liquidation of the Communist League there came for Marx and Engels a cessation of political activity which lasted for many years. The reaction which had commenced in 1849 was gaining in intensity and reached its climax in 1854. All traces of free political activity were obliterated. Labour unions were strictly forbidden. Free press had perished in the turmoil of 1849. All that was left was the Prussian assembly and even this was frightfully reactionary.

Marx and Engels were confronted now with the very serious question of earning a livelihood. We can hardly visualise the distressing material circumstances in which Marx and Engels were at that time. Engels was too proudly recalcitrant to bow to his rich father with whom he had had violent disagreements. He and Marx tried to find some literary work. But Germany was closed to them. In America they had a chance to write for labour organs, but this was not in the least lucrative. It was a splendid opportunity to work without pay.

It was then that Marx published in an American paper [1] his most inspired piece of historical writing, *The Eighteenth Brumaire of Louis Bonaparte.* In it Marx gave a brilliant study of the February Revolution. Step by step, disentangling difficulties, he traced the determining effects of the

---

[1] *Die Revolution,* published by Joseph Weydemeyer in New York in 1852.

struggle between the classes upon the fate of the revolution. He showed how various portions of the bourgeoisie, including the most democratic ones, had one after another, some knowingly and maliciously, and others unwillingly and with tears in their eyes, been betraying and selling the proletariat, casting it forth as prey for generals and executioners. He showed how conditions had been gradually prepared so that a vapid nonentity like Napoleon III was able to seize power.

Meanwhile Marx's material straits were aggravated. During his first years of residence in London he lost two children, a boy and a girl. When the latter died, there was literally no money with which to meet the funeral expenses.

Grinding his teeth, Engels decided to resume his old "dog's trade," as he used to call business. Having found employment in the office of the English branch of his father's factory, he moved to Manchester. At the beginning he was a simple employee. He had still to win the confidence of his father and of the English branch of the firm; he had to prove that he was able to engage himself in a business enterprise.

Marx stayed in London. The Communist League was no more. Only a small number of workers remained clustering about the Communist Workers' Educational Society and eking out a precarious living as tailors and compositors. Only at the end of 1851 an opportunity to write for the *New York Tribune* suddenly presented itself to Marx. The *New York Tribune* was then one of the most influential papers. Charles Dana, one of the editors of the *Tribune,* who had been in Germany and who had met Marx during the Revolution of 1848, invited Marx to write a series of articles on Germany for the paper.* Dana had been in Cologne and he knew the important position Marx occupied among the German journalists. Having taken to heart the interests of his German readers (German immigration into the United States during the Revolution had greatly increased), Dana decided for their benefit to enlarge the section of the *Tribune* dealing with Western Europe. This unforeseen invitation brought in its train some embarrassments, for at that time Marx was not yet able to write English. He turned to Engels for help, and a very curious form of collaboration was established. We have already seen that the *Communist Manifesto*, though it appeared under the joint names of Marx and Engels, was overwhelmingly the work of Marx. Engels' contribution to it was almost as little as had been his contribution to their common work, *The Holy Family*. Now it was Engels who performed the major task. His articles were later collected into a separate volume called *Revolution and Counter-Revolution in Germany*. Marx was credited with this book, but from their correspondence we now know that Engels was the author. However, ideologically it was the common work of Marx and Engels. The latter wrote it on the basis of ideas and facts that were supplied by Marx, and chiefly on the basis of the articles which they had both been writing for the *Neue Rheinische Zeitung*. Thus began Marx's relations with the *New York Tribune*. One year later he gained sufficient mastery of the English language to be able to write his own articles.

Thus from 1852 Marx had a periodical publication in which he could express his views. Unfortunately, it was not in Europe. The American readers sought from it answers to their own specific questions. Though interested in European events, they were interested in them only insofar as they affected events in the United States of America. In the fifties the most vital, the most absorbing question in the United States was the abolition of slavery. Another burning question was that of free trade as it affected the southern and the northern states.

The *New York Tribune* was an abolitionist paper. But in the free-trade vs. protectionism controversy it stood for a most thoroughgoing protectionism. On the question of slavery Marx was in full accord with this paper. On the second issue Marx could not accept the point of view of the editors. But Europe supplied sufficient material on other subjects.

From the Spring of 1853 the tempo of events in Europe began to be accelerated. This acceleration, we must observe, was not caused by any pressure from below. On the contrary, a number of the chief European states, such as Russia, France and England, which were all alike interested in the preservation of order, suddenly began to quarrel. This is characteristic of ruling classes and ruling nations. As soon as they became freed of the dread of revolution, old misunderstandings that had existed among the states of Germany, France, England and Russia again began to rise to the surface. The rivalry, which had been raging among the nations before the Revolution of 1848 and which had only for a time, and through the stress of necessity, been smothered to give place to a common alliance for the suppression of revolution, now flared up again. Russia, who had so successfully helped to restore "order" in western Europe, now seemed to be demanding compensation for her services. She seemed to think that now was the most opportune moment for stretching her paws out to the Balkan peninsula. Her former aspirations gradually to acquire the Turkish dominions in Europe were revived. The clique around the throne of Nicholas I, who deemed this moment auspicious for an aggressive policy, were growing in influence. They hoped that France would not be in a position to offer resistance, and that England, where the Tories were in power, would not interfere, considering the cordial agreement which existed between England and Russia. Thus began the controversy ostensibly about the keys to the Saviour's tomb. In reality the Dardanelles was the bone of contention.

A few months had passed, and the situation became so acute that England and France, both unwilling to fight, both feeling that a war could lead to nothing good, were finally forced to declare war upon Russia. The notorious Crimean War which again brought the Eastern question to the front broke out. Marx and Engels now had their opportunity, even though it was in remote America, to interpret the events of the day. Marx and Engels hailed the war. For, after all, the war did mean that the three major powers which had been the mainstay of counter-revolution, had fallen out, and when thieves fall out, honest folks are likely to benefit by it. It was from this angle that Marx and Engels viewed the war. Yet they had to assume a definite attitude with regard to each of the warring parties.

It is worthwhile dwelling upon this a little longer, for the position which Marx and Engels had taken in the fifties has been repeatedly cited as a precedent in the discussions of tactics in relation to war. It is generally assumed that during the Crimean War, Marx and Engels had placed themselves directly on the side of Turkey, and against Russia. We know the great significance that Marx and Engels had attached to Russian Czarism as the prop of European reaction, and the great significance they had attached to a war against Russia as a factor which would be likely to stir the revolutionary energies of Germany. It was natural, then, for them to have welcomed the war against Russia, and to have subjected Russia to a most scathing criticism. (In their literary collaboration Engels wrote the articles covering the military side of the war, while Marx dealt with the diplomatic and economic questions.)

Does it follow, however, that Marx and Engels had placed themselves on the side of culture, ·enlightenment, and progress as against Russia, and that, having declared themselves against Russia, they *ipso facto* stood for the enlightened and cultured Englishmen and Frenchmen? It would be erroneous to make such a deduction. England and France came in for as much denunciation as Russia. All the efforts of Napoleon and Palmerston to represent the war as a crusade of civilisation and progress against Asiatic barbarism were exposed in the most merciless manner. As to Marx having been a Turcophile, there is nothing more absurd than such an accusation. Neither Marx nor Engels had his eyes closed to the fact that Turkey was even more Asiatic and more barbarous than Russia. They subjected to severe criticism all the countries involved, and they showed no partiality. They had only one criterion—did or did not any given event, any circumstance under discussion, expedite the coming of the revolution? It was from this point of view that they criticised the conduct of England and France which, as we have pointed out, had been reluctantly drawn into this war and thoroughly disgruntled with the obstinate Nicholas I, who flatly refused to consider any compromises that they proffered him. The fears of the ruling classes were fully justified; the war seemed to drag on. It had been started in 1854 and it was terminated in 1856 with the Treaty of Paris. In England and in France, among the masses of workers and peasants, this war caused great excitement. It compelled Napoleon and the ruling classes of England to make a great many promises and concessions. The war ended with the victory of France, England and Turkey. To Russia the Crimean War gave the impetus for the so-called "great reforms." It proved how a state based on the antiquated system of serfdom was incapable of fighting capitalistically developed countries. Russia was forced to consider the emancipation of the serfs.

One more jolt was needed finally to stir a Europe which had fallen into a state of coma after the explosive 1848-1849 epoch. Let us recall thát Marx and Engels, when they broke away from the Willich-Schapper group, had declared that a new revolution was only possible as the result of a fresh powerful economic shock, and that just as the Revolution of 1848 had resulted from the crisis of 1847, so would the new revolution come only as the result of a new economic crisis. The industrial boom that had started in 1849, acquired such a sweep toward the early fifties that even the Crimean War was not able to inflict a serious blow to it.

It began to appear almost as if this boom would be of endless duration. Marx and Engels were confident in 1851 that the next crisis was due not later than 1853. On the basis of their past researches, primarily those of Engels, they held to the opinion that crises were periodic dislocations in the realm of capitalist production, and that they recurred at from five to seven-year intervals. According to this estimate, the crisis which was to follow the one of 1847 was to be expected about 1853. But Marx and Engels made a slight error. The period within which capitalist production goes through the various phases of rising and falling proved to be longer. A panic broke out only in 1857; it assumed unheard-of dimensions, so malignant and widespread did it become.

Marx rapturously greeted this crisis, though to him personally it brought nothing but privation. The income which Marx had been deriving from the *New York Tribune* was not particularly imposing; at first ten and later fifteen dollars per article. Still, in comparison with the first years of his sojourn in London, this income plus the assistance from Engels, who used to take upon himself a great deal of the work for the American newspapers, gave him a chance to make both ends meet. He could even find time, despite his constant working on *Capital*, to write, without remuneration, articles for the central Chartist organ, the *People's Paper*.

With the panic of 1857, conditions grew considerably worse. The United States was the first to suffer. The *New York Tribune* had to reduce its expenses; foreign correspondence was reduced to a minimum. Marx again became encumbered with debts and again had to look for sporadic earnings. This lean period lasted until 1859. Then came a

respite.   Finally, in 1862, Marx's work for the *Tribune* came
to an end.

But if in his personal affairs Marx was unfortunate (during this period other misfortunes fell upon him), in his revolutionary outlook he never was more optimistic than after
the year 1857.   As he had foreseen, the new economic crisis
brought to life a number of revolutionary movements all over
the world.   The abolition of slavery in America and the
emancipation of the serfs in Russia became most crucial
problems which demanded immediate solution.   Bourgeois
England had to strain all her resources in her struggle with
the vast uprisings in India.   Western Europe too was in a
state of commotion.

The Revolution of 1848 had left a few unanswered questions.   Italy remained disunited.   A large section of her
northern territory remained in the hands of Austria.   Hungary was crushed with the aid of Russian bayonets and was
again chained to Austria.   Germany persisted as a heap of
principalities and kingdoms of different magnitudes, where
Prussia and Austria had been incessantly bickering and
fighting for dominance, for the so-called hegemony in the
union of German states.

In 1858 there already began a general rise of the opposition and revolutionary movements in all western European
countries.   The old unsolved problems were again brought
to the fore.   In Germany the strife for unification asserted
itself once more.   The struggle between the party which
wanted a Great Germany, which clamoured for the unification of the whole of Germany including Austria, and the
"Little German" party which demanded that Prussia be the
point around which all the German states with the exception of Austria be united, was still going on.

In Italy there was an analogous awakening of national
aspirations.   In France the panic of 1857 brought in its
train the ruin of many inflated enterprises; it affected par-

ticularly the textile industries. The petty-bourgeoisie began to show a spirit of opposition. A new vigour was also manifested by the underground revolutionary organisations. The labour movement which had become moribund after the June defeat, was revivified, particularly in the building and the furniture-making trades. Russia, too, received its first capitalist baptism in a series of colossal business failures in Moscow; it now began to hobble along the path of liberal reforms.

To rid themselves of internal difficulties the governments, and first of all Napoleon, endeavoured to distract the attention of their peoples by starting up a tinsel show in external politics. Napoleon was reminded by the attempt of the Italian revolutionist Orsini, in 1858, that the police was not always omnipotent. He was forced to take into consideration the popular discontent. To dissipate the revolutionary sentiment of the labouring masses, Napoleon raised the progressive slogan of liberating Italy from the Austrian yoke. He immediately entered into secret agreements with Cavour, the minister of the Sardinian king. The rôle played by Sardinia in Italy was analogous to that of Prussia in Germany.

While the babble of the official press implied that it was all a question of unifying Italy, the actual agreement, upon the basis of which Napoleon had promised to help Sardinia, had an entirely different content; it was not the unification of Italy but the rounding out of Sardinia which was promised Lombardy and Venice. Besides the promise that the Papal Dominions would be left intact, Napoleon was to receive as compensation Nice and Savoy. Napoleon, who was compelled to wriggle between opposition from the left and the clerical party, did not want to quarrel with the Pope and was therefore against an actual unification of Italy. On the other hand, he hoped that the acquisition of two new territories would satisfy the French patriots.

Thus arose a new and an extremely important political question which perturbed all Europe and especially the revolutionists within the different countries. What attitude were the revolutionists and socialists to assume? Were they to side with Napoleon who had stepped forth almost as a revolutionist, who was advocating the liberal principle of the right of Italy to self-determination, or were they to be on the side of Austria which was the personification of despotism, which was the oppressor of Italy and Hungary? This was a question of supreme importance. The different answers to this question dictated the different tactics of such revolutionists as Marx and Engels on one side, and Ferdinand Lassalle (1825-1864) on the other.

Until now we had no occasion to mention Lassalle, though he had been one of the first disciples of Marx and had already taken part in the events of 1848. We shall not dwell on his biography, for it would lead us too much astray from our main topic. During the fifties, after having served a short term in prison, Lassalle stayed in Germany and continued his scientific work, keeping up his relations with Marx and Engels at the same time. In 1859, a controversy between them arose in connection with the Italian question. This was an extremely interesting polemic, and the two sides to this controversy were finally crystallised into two factions within the same party. The disagreements were reduced to the following:

Napoleon III and his clique were great adepts at shaping public opinion. Just as during the Crimean War, the market was flooded with a great mass of booklets and pamphlets in which the liberalism of Napoleon and the justice of the Italian cause were most eloquently championed. Many voluntary and a much greater number of mercenary journalists joined this literary campaign. The volunteers were re-

cruited chiefly from among the Hungarian and the Polish
emigrants. Just as they had, a few years before, regarded
the Crimean War as a war of progress and civilisation
against Asiatic despotism and had formed and equipped
legions of volunteers in order to aid Palmerston and Napoleon, so did the Hungarian and Polish emigrants, with very
few exceptions, maintain now that Napoleon was fighting for
progress and for the self-determination of nations, and that
it was incumbent upon all forward-looking people to hasten
to his aid. These emigrants, among whom there were many
who did not disdain Napoleon's money, entered the Italo-
French army.

Neither was Austria slumbering. She financed the publicists who were trying to prove that in this war Austria was
defending the interests of all of Germany, that in case
Napoleon conquered Austria, he could seize the Rhine, that
if this were the case, it was really Germany and not Italy
that Austria was concerned with, that, therefore Austria's
retention of her dominion over Northern Italy was for the
purpose of protecting Germany.

These were the two main channels in which the opinions of
European journalism of the time were coursing. In Germany itself the problem was complicated by the controversy
between the "Great-Germany" and the "Little-Germany"
parties. It was quite natural that the Great-Germanists
who wanted the unification of the whole of Germany, Austria
included, should lean to the side of the latter, while the Little-
Germanists, who pulled toward Prussia, should maintain that
Austria be left to her own fate. Of course, there were various shadings, but these did not essentially change the
general picture.

What then were the attitudes taken by Marx and Engels
on the one hand, and by Lassalle on the other? They all held
to the principles of the *Communist Manifesto*. During the
Revolution of 1848 they had all declared themselves in favour

of a United German Republic, with the German districts of
Austria incorporated. It seemed that there was no place for
any disagreements. In reality these differences were not
any less profound than the differences which arose among
the various Social-Democrats who stood on the same Marxian
platform at the beginning of the Great War in 1914.

Marx and Engels, in their articles and pamphlets, reasoned that in order to protect the Rhine, Germany was not
in need of Northern Italy, and that it could very well afford
to permit Austria to give up all its Italian possessions to a
United Italy, that any attempt to support Austria, sup-
posedly in the interests of Germany, meant a compromise
with Austrian despotism.

Marx and Engels were consistent. They attacked Napoleon as relentlessly as they lashed Austrian and Prussian reaction. A complete victory for Napoleon, they felt, would
be as much of a calamity as a complete victory for Austria.
Engels maintained that Napoleon, should he defeat Austria,
would also attack Germany. He therefore advanced the idea
that the unification of Italy as well as that of Germany
should be accomplished by forces within these countries themselves. Revolutionists, according to him, could not consistently support either side. The only thing for them to
consider should be the interests of the proletarian revolution. We must not overlook another factor which was loom-
ing behind the stage. Engels was pointing out, and justly,
that Napoleon would not have dared to declare war upon
Austria had he not been confident of the silent consent of
Russia, had he not been assured that she would not go to the
aid of Austria. He thought it quite probable that in this
there existed some sort of an understanding between France
and Russia. During the Crimean War, Austria had repaid
in "base ingratitude" that same Russia which had so "self-
sacrificingly" and so "unselfishly" helped her to strangle the
Hungarian revolution. Russia now had obviously no

scruples about punishing Austria with Napoleon's hands. If an agreement between France and Russia actually existed by which Russia promised to come to the aid of France, it would be the duty of Germany to hasten to the assistance of Austria, but it would already be a revolutionary Germany. Then the situation would be similar to that upon which Marx and Engels had been counting in the days of the Revolution of 1848. It would be a war of revolution against reaction. The bourgeois parties would not be able to attract to themselves all the lower classes; they would give way successively to ever-more radical parties, thus creating the opportunity for the victory of the most extreme, the most revolutionary party—the proletarian party.

Such was the point of view of Marx and Engels. Lassalle regarded this question differently. To a degree this difference could be explained by the different objective conditions to which these people were directly exposed. Lassalle lived in Prussia and was too closely bound up with the local Prussian conditions. Marx and Engels lived in England, on the watch-tower of the world; they considered European events from the point of view of the World Revolution, not only the German, nor merely the Prussian.

Lassalle argued in the following manner: To him the most dangerous foe of Germany was the internal foe, Austria. She was a more dangerous enemy than liberal France, or than a Russia which was already in the grip of liberal reforms. Austria was the main cause of the bleak reaction that pressed so insufferably upon Germany. Napoleon, though a usurper, was none the less an expression of liberalism, progress, and civilisation. That was why, Lassalle felt, that in this war the German Democracy should abandon Austria to her own fate, and that the defeat of Austria would be the most desirable outcome.

When we read Lassalle's writings dealing with this question—all the compliments he showered upon Napoleon and

Russia, the extreme caution he displayed in discussing official Prussia—we are compelled to make an effort so as not to become confused. We constantly have to remind ourselves that Lassalle tried to speak as a Prussian democrat who wanted to convince the ruling class of Prussia, the Junkers, that no aid should be granted to Austria. But, having donned the cloak of a Prussian democrat, Lassalle really expounded his own ideas which diverged sharply from those of Marx and Engels. Later this divergence took on a graver aspect. Carried away by the desire to attain immediate and tangible success, determined to become a "practical politician," instead of a doctrinaire, he allowed himself to resort to arguments and proofs which placed him under obligations to the ruling party, which inveigled him into flattering those whom he tried to persuade to leave Austria without assistance. Abuse hurled upon Austria, a gentle attitude toward Russia, the coquetting with official Prussia —all this was so far only the enthusiasm of a publicist who was not writing in the name of the party. The same tactics, however, when they were subsequently carried over by Lassalle into the immediate practical struggle, became fraught with danger.

The war between France and Austria terminated differently from what either side expected. At the beginning, Austria, opposed by a lonely Italy, was unequivocally victorious. Later she was defeated by the combined forces of France and Italy. But as soon as the war began to assume a popular character and to threaten an actual revolutionary unification of Italy and the abolition of the Papal district, Napoleon accepted Russian mediation and hurried to crawl out of the war. Sardinia had to be satisfied with Lombardy. Venice remained in the hands of Austria. To compensate himself for French blood and French money, Napoleon helped himself to the whole province of Savoy, the birthplace of the Sardinian kings and, to prove to the famous Italian

revolutionist and fighter for a United Italy, Giuseppe Garibaldi (1807-1882), that one must not be misled by the
promises of crowned knaves, he annexed Garibaldi's native
city, Nice, and its environs. Thus did the "liberal" Napoleon with the thunderous applause of liberal fools and
bamboozled revolutionists defend the "right of self-determination" of Italy and other oppressed nationalities. Lassalle, too, was to discover that not only was Napoleon not
better than Austria, but that he could run rings about
Austria when it came to Machiavellian double-dealing.
Italy was left as dismembered as it had been. Only Sardinia became more rounded out. But now something quite
unexpected happened. Owing to the disillusionment and indignation resulting from Napoleon's policies, a strong revolutionary movement was started in Italy. At the head was
the noble revolutionist, but the bad politician, Garibaldi. In
1861, Italy was changed into a United Kingdom, but without
Venice. The further unification of Italy now passed into the
hands of bourgeois business men, Garibaldian renegades and
adventurers.

Marx had to engage in another polemic in connection with
the Franco-Austrian war. We have seen that the entire
German democracy took a definite stand in this conflict between Napoleon and Austria. The most noted and influential man among the German democrats was the old revolutionist, Karl Vogt (1817-1895), who in 1849 had also been
forced to flee to Switzerland. He was not merely active in
politics; he was a great savant with a European reputation.
He is known as one of the chief exponents of naturo-histori-
cal materialism which is so often confused, particularly by
bourgeois scholars, with the historical materialism of Marx
and Engels. His influence was wide, not only among the
German democrats, but also among the international revolutionary emigrants, especially the Polish, Italian and Hungarian. His home at Geneva served as a political centre.

For Napoleon it was extremely important to attract to his side the noted scholar and leader of the German democrats. Because of the overweening vanity of the old German professor, this was easily accomplished. Vogt was on a friendly footing with Napoleon's brother, Prince Plon-Plon,* who acted the part of a great liberal and patron of science— Vogt had been getting money from him for distribution among the representatives of the various emigrant groups.

When our professor came out most decidedly for Napoleon and Italy, it of course created a tremendous impression among the circles of emigrant revolutionists. As always happens in such cases, among the emigrants that were most closely connected with Marx and Engels, there were some who kept up relations with the republican emigrants. One of the latter, Karl Blind, declared in the presence of a few communists that Vogt was receiving money from Napoleon. This was printed in one of the London papers. When Wilhelm Liebknecht (1826-1900), who was correspondent for an Augsburg paper, reported these rumours, Vogt instituted a case for libel and won, for there was no documentary evidence against him.

Jubilant over his victory, Vogt published a special pamphlet about this trial. Being perfectly certain that Wilhelm Liebknecht did not undertake a step, did not write a line without the direction of Marx, Vogt aimed all his blows against the latter. And so this man on the basis of precise data, as he claimed, accused Marx of being at the head of a gang of expropriators and counterfeiters who stopped at nothing. Everything that the imagination of a "sincere" democrat could conjure up was let loose against the communists. A man notorious for his penchant for the comforts of life, Herr Vogt was accusing Marx of living in luxury at the expense of the workers.

Vogt's pamphlet, thanks to the name of the author as well as the name of the man he attacked (Marx had just published his *Critique of Political Economy*), created a sensation and, as was to be expected, met with the most favourable reception from the bourgeois press. The bourgeois journals, and chief of all, the renegade bourgeois scribes who had once known Marx personally, were delighted at the opportunity to spill a pailful of slops upon the head of their old foe.

Personally, Marx was of the opinion that the press had a right to criticise any public man it pleased. It is the privilege, he claimed, of every one who appears publicly, to bear praise or condemnation. You are received with stones and rotten apples? It matters little. Ordinary abuse—and it was flung without end—he absolutely ignored. Only when the interests of the cause demanded it, did he deign to reply. And then he was merciless.

When Vogt's pamphlet appeared, the question of whether or not to answer arose. Lassalle and some other German friends of his circle maintained that the pamphlet ought to be ignored. They saw what a tremendous impression in favour of Vogt was created by the trial he had won. The great democrat, they felt, was inadvertently injured by Liebknecht, and in defending his honour he lost his head a bit. Another trial would only bring him another triumph, for there were no proofs against him. The most advisable thing it seemed, was to ignore him, and to let public opinion become pacified.

Such philistine arguments could not, of course, affect Marx. One could disdain answering personal attacks, but the honour of the party had to be defended. Though Marx and his most intimate friends were convinced that Vogt had really been bribed, they found themselves in a quandary, for both Blind and another emigrant renounced now what they had said, and Liebknecht was placed in a position of a slanderer.

Finally it was decided to answer. An attempt to get Vogt

before a court of justice proved futile because of the partiality of the Prussian courts. The only way out was a literary attack. Marx took upon himself the execution of the
difficult task. We are now approaching a point where we are
again forced to strongly disagree with the late Franz Mehring. In his opinion, Marx could easily have spared himself
a great deal of endless worry and effort, and the waste of
precious time without any use to the great task of his life,
had he simply refused to take any part in the quarrel between Liebknecht and Vogt. But such a course would have
been entirely at variance with Marx's actions.

Mehring overlooked completely the fundamental controversy that had been going on among the emigrants. He did
not discern that behind this, what appeared to be a personal
incident, there were concealed profound tactical disagreements which had sprung up between the proletarian party
and all bourgeois parties, that even within the proletarian
party itself, as the case of Lassalle indicated, there were revealed dangerous oscillations. Nor did Mehring notice that
the book against Vogt contained a criticism of all the arguments of Lassalle and his confrères.

Let us turn to the book *Herr Vogt* itself. From the literary point of view it belongs to the best of Marx's polemical
writings. We should add that in all literature there is no
equal to this book. There was Pascal's famous pamphlet
against the Jesuits. In the literature of the eighteenth century there were Lessing's pamphlets directed against his literary adversaries. But all these, as well as other known
pamphlets, pursued only literary aims.

In *Herr Vogt*, Marx's objective was not merely the political and moral annihilation of a man greatly respected by
the bourgeois world for his scholarly and political attainments. True, this job, too, Marx fulfilled most brilliantly.
All that Marx had were the printed works of Vogt. The star
witnesses retracted their statements. Marx, therefore, took

all the political writings of Vogt and proved that he was a Bonapartist and that he had been literally reiterating all the arguments that were developed in the writings of agents bought by Napoleon. And when Marx came to the conclusion that Vogt was either a self-satisfied parrot idiotically repeating the Bonapartists' arguments or possibly a bought agent like the rest of the Bonapartist publicists, one is ready to believe that by and by history will bring to light Vogt's receipt for the money he received.*

But Marx did not confine himself to political scourging. His pamphlet was not mere abuse interspersed with strong words. Marx also directed at Vogt another weapon of which he was a past master—sarcasm, irony, ridicule. With each chapter, the comical figure of Herr Vogt was brought into greater relief. We see how the great savant and the great political worker is converted into a boastful, garrulous Falstaff, prone to have a gay time on some one else's money.

But behind Vogt there loomed the most influential part of the German bourgeois democracy. Marx, therefore, also exposed the political miserliness of this "flower" of the German nation, bearing down upon the heads of those who, in spite of their proximity to the communist camp, could not free themselves of obsequiousness before the "learned ones."

Vogt's base attempt to pour filth upon the neediest and most radical faction of the revolutionary emigrants afforded Marx the opportunity of drawing the picture of the "moral" and "proper" bourgeois parties, those who were in power as well as those in opposition, and particularly, of characterising the prostituted press of the bourgeois world, which had become a capitalist enterprise deriving a profit from the sale of words, as some enterprises derive it from the sale of manure.

Even in Marx's lifetime, students of the decade between 1849-1859 acknowledged that there was no other work that had such an insight into the parties of this epoch as did this work of Marx. A present-day reader, no doubt, would need many commentaries to grasp all the details, but anyone would easily understand the political significance that Marx's pamphlet had at the time.

Lassalle himself had to admit that Marx wrote a masterpiece, that all fears had been idle, that Vogt was forever compromised as a political leader.

In the late fifties and the early sixties, when a new movement had started among the petty-bourgeoisie and the working class, when the struggle for influence upon the urban poor was becoming more intensified, it became important to establish that not only were the representatives of the proletarian democracy intellectually not inferior to the most outstanding figures of the bourgeois democracy, but that they were infinitely superior. In the person of Vogt, the bourgeois democrats received a mortal blow to the prestige of one of its acknowledged leaders. It remained for Lassalle to be thankful to Marx for the latter's making it easier for him to carry on the fight against the progressives for the influence upon the German workers.

We shall now pass to an examination of a most interesting question—the attitude of Marx and Engels toward Lassalle's revolutionary agitation. We have already indicated that Lassalle began his agitation in 1862, when the conflict pertaining to the method of fighting the government became very sharp within the ranks of the Prussian bourgeois democracy. It happened that in 1858, the old Prussian King who had so notoriously distinguished himself during the 1848 Revolution, became completely and hopelessly insane. Wilhelm, the "grapeshot prince," who had achieved infamy by his slaughter of the democrats in 1849 and 1850, was first appointed Regent and finally King. At the beginning he felt compelled to strike up a liberal tune, but very soon he found himself at odds with the Assembly on the question of army organisation. The government insisted on in-

creasing the army and demanded heavier taxation, the liberal bourgeoisie demanded definite guarantees and the con-
trolling power. On the basis of this budget conflict, problems of tactics arose. Lassalle, personally still closely bound
up with the democratic and progressive bourgeois circles,
demanded more decisive tactics. Since every constitution is
only an expression of the factual interrelation of forces in a
given society, it was necessary to initiate the movement of a
new social force directed against the government, headed by
the determined and clever reactionary Bismarck.

What this new social force was, Lassalle pointed out in a
special report which he read before the workers. Devoted
to a presentation of the "connection existing between the contemporary historical epoch with the idea of the working
class" it is better known by the name of *The Workingmen's
Programme*. In substance it was an exposition of the fundamental ideas of the *Communist Manifesto*, considerably di-
luted and adapted to the legal conditions of the time. Still,
since the Revolution of 1848, it was the first open declaration of the necessity of organising the working class into an
independent political organisation sharply marked off from
all, even the most democratic, bourgeois parties.

Lassalle thus stepped forth to meet the movement which
arose independently and grew very rapidly among the workers of Saxony, where strife had already sprung up among
the democrats and the few representatives of the "old guard"
of the proletarian movement of 1848. Among these workers
the idea of calling together a congress of workers was
already being debated. A special committee was organised
at Leipzig for this purpose. Having been called upon by this
committee to declare himself upon the questions of the aims
and the problems of the working-class movement, Lassalle
developed his programme in his *Open Letter* addressed to
the Leipzig committee.

After subjecting to a severe criticism the programme of

the bourgeois progressives and the means they were pro-
posing for the amelioration of the workers' conditions, Lassalle advanced the idea of the indispensability of the
organisation of an independent party of the working class.
The principal political demand, upon the realisation of
which all the forces had to concentrate, was the winning of
universal suffrage. As to his economic programme, Lassalle,
relying upon what he called the "iron law of wages," proved
that there were no means of raising wages above a definite
minimum. He therefore recommended the organisation of
producing co-operatives with the aid of credits granted by the
government.

It is obvious that Marx could not accept such a plan.
Lassalle's efforts to draw Marx to his side proved futile.
There were other reasons which took on definite form only
a few months later when Lassalle, carried away by "practical politics" and his struggle against the progressive party,
almost stooped to a flirtation with the government.

At any rate, it is beyond any shadow of a doubt—and this
was recognised by Marx himself—that it was Lassalle who
after the prolonged spell of reaction from 1849 to 1862
planted the proletarian banner on German soil, that it was
he who was the first organiser of the German working-class
party. This was Lassalle's undeniable service.

But in Lassalle's very intensive though short-lived—it
lasted less than two years—organisational and political activity there were radical defects which, even more than his
inadequate programme, were bound to repel Marx and
Engels.

It was very conspicuous that not only did Lassalle not
underline the connection between the General German Labour
Union which he organised and the old communist movement,
but, on the contrary, most vehemently denied any connection.* Having borrowed most of his basic ideas from the
Communist Manifesto and other works of Marx, he most

diligently avoided any reference to them. Only in one of his very last works does he quote Marx, not the communist, not the revolutionist, but the economist.

Lassalle explained this by tactical considerations. He did not wish to frighten away the insufficiently conscious masses which had to be freed from the spiritual custody of the progressives, who continued spreading fairy tales of the terrible spectre of communism.

Lassalle was vainglorious; he loved all kinds of din, parade, and advertisement which act so powerfully on the uncultivated mass, and which repel the educated worker. He enjoyed being depicted as the creator of the German labour movement. It was this that repelled not only Marx and Engels but also all the veterans of the old revolutionary movement. It is significant that only the former Weitlingites and Marx's factional opponents joined Lassalle. Not one year had passed ere the German workers discovered that their movement was started not by Lassalle alone. Marx and his friends protested against this desire to liquidate all bonds with the old revolutionary and underground movement. This reluctance to compromise himself by his connections with the old illegal group was also explained by Lassalle's weakness for *real politik*.

The other point of disagreement was the question of universal suffrage. This demand had been advanced by the Chartists. Marx and Engels had also been propounding it, but they could not recognise the exaggerated importance which Lassalle was attaching to it, or the arguments which he was advancing. With him it became a miracle-working panacea, sufficient in itself, and which independently of other changes in the political and economic life would immediately place the power in the hands of the workers. He naïvely believed that the workers would win about ninety per cent of all the seats in Parliament once they had the vote. He did not understand that a number of very important conditions were prerequisite for the rendering of universal suffrage into a means for class education instead of a means for the deception of the masses.

Not less profound was the disagreement as to the question of "producers' associations." For Marx and Engels they were then already a subsidiary means of very limited significance. They were to serve as proof that neither the entrepreneur nor the capitalist was an indispensable factor in production. But to view co-operative associations as a means for a gradual taking over by society of the collective means of production, was to forget that in order to accomplish this it was necessary first to be in possession of political power. Only then, as had been indicated in the *Manifesto*, could a series of necessary measures be effected.

Just as sharply did Marx and Engels disagree with Lassalle on the rôle of trade unions. Completely overestimating the significance of co-operative producers' associations, Lassalle considered as absolutely useless the organisation of trade unions, and in this respect he harked back to the views of the old utopians who had been subjected to a most thorough criticism in Marx's *Poverty of Philosophy*.

Not less profound and, from the practical side, even more important was the disagreement in the domain of tactics. We have not the least right to accuse Marx, as did Mehring, of overestimating the significance of the progressives, of placing too great a hope in the bourgeoisie. We have already had occasion to read Marx's characterisation of the Prussian bourgeoisie written by him as a result of the experiences of 1848. We have seen how severely he criticised the bourgeois democracy in his polemic against Vogt. The difference arose not because Marx, torn away from his native land, still retained faith in the progressivism of the Prussian bourgeoisie, while Lassalle, better acquainted with Prussian realities, was thoroughly disillusioned in them. It was a disagreement concerning the tactics in relation to the bourgeoisie. Just as in a war between capitalist states, so in the struggle between the progressive bourgeoisie and Bismarck, was it necessary to work out tactics which would remove the danger of the socialists becoming catspaws of one of the conflicting parties. In his onslaught against the Prussian progressives, Lassalle was forgetting that there was still a Prussian feudalism, a Prussian Junkerdom, which was not less inimical to the workers than the bourgeoisie. He beat and lashed the progressives with good reason, but he did keep himself within the necessary bounds and only compromised his cause by toadying before the government. Lassalle did not even hesitate to resort to wholly unpermissible compromises. When, for instance, some workers were arrested, he suggested that they address a petition to Bismarck, who, no doubt, would release them just to spite the liberals. The workers refused to follow Lassalle's advice. A study of his speeches, particularly those delivered during the first half of the year 1864, reveals a multitude of such errors. We shall not dwell on the negotiations which Lassalle, without the knowledge of the organisation, was conducting with Bismarck, thus exposing his own reputation and the cause which he served to serious injury.

These were the differences which prevented Marx and Engels from giving the authority of their names in support of Lassalle's agitation. But—and this we emphasise—while refusing Lassalle their support, they nevertheless refused to oppose him openly. Their influence upon their co-workers in Germany, Liebknecht, for instance, was in the same spirit. Meanwhile Lassalle, who greatly prized their neutrality, was precipitously rolling down an inclined plane. Liebknecht, as well as other comrades from Berlin, and the Rhine province, was demanding of Marx to come out openly against Lassalle's erroneous tactics. It is quite likely that it would have come to an open rupture had not Lassalle been killed on August 30, 1864.   Four weeks after his death, September 28, 1864, the First International was founded. This gave Marx a chance to return to immediate revolutionary work, this time on an international scale.

CHAPTER VII

WE pointed out in the previous chapter that almost ten
years had gone by before the revolutionary labour movement
began to recover from its defeat of 1848-49. We showed
that the beginning of this recovery was bound up with the
crisis of 1857-58 which was assuming international proportions and which even affected Russia in a very pronounced
form. We indicated how the ruling classes of Europe, outwardly peaceful up to that time, were forced to undertake
anew the solution of all those problems which were put
forward by the Revolution of 1848 and never solved. The
most important problem pressing for a solution was that of
nationalism—the unification of Italy, the formation of a
united Germany. We mentioned briefly the fact that this
revolutionary movement was, strictly speaking, limited only
to Western Europe and influenced strongly only a part of
England, but that it failed to reach the major part of
Europe, Russia, and the far-away United States of America.
In Russia, at that time, the burning question of the day was
the abolition of serfdom. It was the so-called period of
"great reforms" when the movement began which, towards
the early sixties, shaped itself into those underground revolutionary societies the foremost of which was the so-called
Land and Freedom society. On the other side of the At-
lantic, in the United States, the question of the abolition

of slavery was being pressed for solution. This question, even in a greater measure than the similar one in Russia, showed how really international the world had become, the world which used to be thought of in terms of a limited part of Europe.

A problem so far removed as that of the abolition of slavery in the United States became of the utmost importance to Europe itself. Indeed, so important did it become that Marx, in his foreword to the first volume of *Capital,* stated that the war for the abolition of slavery sounded the tocsin for the new labour movement in Western Europe.

We shall begin with the most important labour movement, the English. Of the old revolutionary Chartist movement there was nothing left by 1863. Chartism was dead. Indeed some historians maintain that it died in 1848, right after the famous experiment of the abortive demonstration. But actually Chartism had one more period of bloom in the fifties, during the Crimean War. Owing to the leadership of Ernest Jones (1819-1868), a splendid orator and a brilliant journalist, who had built up with the assistance of Marx and Marx's friends the best socialist organ of those times, Chartism was able to utilise the discontent of the masses of workers during the Crimean War. There were months when the *People's Paper,* the central organ of the Chartists, was one of the most influential papers. Marx's masterly articles directed at Gladstone and particularly at Palmerston were attracting universal attention. But this was only a temporary revival. Soon after the conclusion of the war, the Chartists lost their organ. The causes lay not only in the factional dissensions which flared up between Jones and his opponents; there were more basic causes.

The first cause was the amazing efflorescence of English industry which had begun as far back as 1849. The minor irritations which were occurring during this period, irritations in separate branches of industry, did not in the least interfere with the general rise of industry as a whole. The vast number of unemployed at the end of the forties was completely dissolved in this great industrial overflow. It may well be said that for many decades, nay, for centuries, English industry was not in so great a need of workers as after the first half of the nineteenth century. The second cause was the powerful wave of emigration from England to the United States and Australia, where inexhaustible gold mines were discovered between the years 1851 and 1855. In the course of a few years, two million workers emigrated from England. As is usual in such cases, the emigrants were not drawn from among the children and the aged; the healthiest, most energetic, and the strongest elements were leaving England. The working-class movement and the Chartist movement were being drained of the reserve from which they were drawing their strength. These were the two primary causes. There were also a number of secondary causes.

Concurrent with the weakening of the Chartist movement, there was a general loosening of the ties which held the various branches of the movement together. Even in the forties a struggle had been going on between the trade union and the Chartist movements. Now other forms of the working-class movement, too, developed separatist tendencies and were attempting to desert the parent trunk. The co-operatives, for example, were developing on the basis of certain historical conditions of the English labour movement. This peculiarity of the English labour movement was becoming well-defined even in the fifties. We often encounter in its history various special organisations of sudden rapid growth and of still more sudden and still more rapid decay. Some of these organisations comprised hundreds of thousands of members. One, for instance, had as its goal the abolition of drunkenness. The Chartist organisation was always following the line of least resistance. At first it tried to conduct the war against alcohol within the boundaries of party organisations. It then began to view it as a special goal; it organised special societies all over England, thus diverting from the main labour movement a number of battalions. Besides this teetotaler movement, there was the co-operative movement led by the so-called Christian Socialists. Joseph Stephens (1805-1879), the famous revolutionary minister, was one of the most popular orators of the forties, but he subsequently turned considerably to the right. Stephens was joined by a number of similar elements drawn from among philanthropists and well-wishers who were preaching practical Christianity to the workers. This indicated the decline of the Chartist movement as a political factor. It devoted itself to the forming of co-operative societies. Since this movement was not menacing to the ruling classes, it was helped even by members of the governing party. Several members of the intelligentsia who commiserated with the working class, attached themselves to the movement. Thus in pursuit of its special aims, another branch of the working class broke away.

We shall not enumerate the different forms and ramifications of these movements. Let us examine the trade unions. True, at the beginning of the fifties the trade-union movement did not meet with conditions as favourable to its development, as did the co-operative and the teetotaler movements. None the less it encountered less resistance than had the old Chartist movement. In 1851 the first stable union of the English machine-making trades was organised. This union was headed by two energetic workers who succeeded in repressing the typically English craft spirit according to which it was customary to form trade unions within the confines of one or two towns or, at the most, one or two counties. We should not, of course, overlook the peculiarities of English industry. It was difficult to transform the union of textile workers into a national union for the simple reason that the major part of the textile industry was concentrated in a very small area. Almost all of the textile workers in England were huddled together in two counties. Thus a two-county union was equivalent to a national union. The chief trouble of the English trade unions was due not so much to their local limitations as to their craft traditions. Each separate craft within the same industry was invariably prone to organise an independent union. This was why trade unionism was unable, despite its very vigorous start, to create forms of organisation equal to the task of directing a struggle against the owners of large-scale industries. While industry was flourishing, the overwhelming majority of the workers easily won increased wages. What is more, since there were not enough workers to fill the needs of the expanding new industries, the owners, in order to attract more workers, competed among themselves and were therefore ready to meet the workers more than half way. The English capitalists, during these years, tried to lure workers from the continent—Germans, Frenchmen, Belgians—into their country.

Under such circumstances, the trade-union movement, despite its growth, was bound to remain on a lower plane of development. Separate trade unions, which were formed in different subdivisions of one and the same branch of industry, remained disconnected, not only within the boundaries of the whole country but even within the confines of one town. There were not even any local councils.

The crisis of 1857-1858 brought vast changes into this atmosphere. As we have seen, the best-organised trade union was the union of the skilled machine-making workers. Like the textile industry, the manufacture of machines was one of those few industries which did not produce exclusively for the home market. Beginning with the fifties the manufacture of textiles and machines became the privileged branches of industry, for they maintained a monopoly on

the world market.   The skilled workers in these industries
easily won concessions from the employers who were reap-
ing enormous profits.   Thus it was that in these two branches
of industry conditions of "civil peace" between the workers
and the employers were beginning to be established.   The
effects of the very acute crisis were rapidly disappearing.
The gulf separating the skilled from the unskilled workers
was becoming ever wider.   This, in its turn, had debilitating
results on any strike movements in these industries.

Still, not all the workers were so pacific.   The crisis was
chiefly reflected on the building trades and on the workers
engaged in these trades. Henceforth the workers in the building trades occupied the first ranks in the struggles of the
English workers.

The growth of capitalism brought in its train an unprece-
dented swelling of the urban population and consequently
a greater demand for living quarters.   Hence the great boom
in the building industries.   In the forties England was in
the throes of a railroad fever, in the early fifties a building
fever took its place.   Houses were built by the thousand.
They were in every sense of the word thrown upon the
market like any other commodity.   The building business
though as yet little developed technically, had already fallen
into the hands of big capitalists.   The English building
contractor would rent a large plot of land upon which he
would build hundreds of houses which he would either rent
or sell.

The development of the building industry lured a multitude of workers from the villages—woodworkers, carpenters,
painters, masons, paperhangers, in brief, all kinds of workers who were engaged in the building, decorating and fur-
nishing of homes.   With the growth of building there was a
corresponding boom in the furniture, paperhanging and
artistic trades.   The increase in the population gave impetus

to the development of large-scale shoemaking and clothing industries.

Thus the crisis of 1857-1858 had a particularly strong repercussion in these new branches of capitalist production. Great masses were left without work, and a reserve army of unemployed, which made its pressure felt on the workers in the shops and factories, was formed. The employers on their part did not hesitate to make use of this weapon to oppress the workers, to cut down their wages, and lengthen the working day. But the workers, to the great surprise of their employers, answered this with a general strike in 1859, which became one of the greatest strikes London had known. As if further to increase the surprise of the employers, the strike of the building trades found strong support in other bodies of workers in all branches of industry. This strike attracted the attention of Europe no less than the important political events of that day. In connection with it many meetings and miscellaneous gatherings took place. Among the speakers we often come across the name of Cremer. At a meeting in Hyde Park, Cremer declared that the strike of the building trades is but the first skirmish between the economics of labour and that of capital. Other workers such as George Odger (1820-1877), for instance, also carried on much propaganda work. Leaflets, as well, played a part in the agitation. Thus the famous colloquy between the labourer and the capitalist found in the first volume of *Capital*—one of the most brilliant pages of that book—is in places almost a word-for-word repetition of one of the propaganda leaflets printed by the workers during the strike of 1859-1860.*

As a result of this strike, which soon ended in a compromise, there arose in London for the first time, the Trades Council, at the head of which stood the three chief leaders, Odger, Cremer and George Howell; they are also the ones whom we meet at the first General Council of the First Inter-

national.   Already, in 1861, this London Trades Council
had become one of the most influential labour organisations.
At the same time, like the first Soviets, it was taking on a
political character.   It endeavoured to react to all the
events affecting the working class.   Using this as a model,
similar trades councils were formed in many other places in
England and Scotland.   Thus in 1862, class organisations
of workers again came into being.   These trades councils
were the outstanding political and economic centres of the
day.

When we turn to France we see that the crisis there was
no less severe.   It reacted strongly not only on the textile
industry but also on all the other industries for which Paris
was then famous.   We have already mentioned the fact that
the purpose of the war undertaken by Napoleon in 1859 was
to sidetrack this growing discontent of the working class.
Towards the beginning of the sixties this crisis affected
especially those specifically Parisian trades known as the
artistic trades.   But Paris was also an important urban
centre; it had been undergoing a strong and steady development.   One of the major reforms carried through by
Napoleon was the rebuilding of several residential districts
in Paris.   Old narrow streets were raised, broad avenues were
laid out, making the erection of barricades thus impossible.
This building activity brought about the same results here
as it had in London, namely, an enormous increase in the
number of workers engaged in the building trades.   Indeed,
it is these building trades with their various subdivisions
ranging from the unskilled to the highly skilled on the one
hand, and the workers engaged in the manufacture of articles
of luxury—the representatives of the artistic trades—on
the other hand, who supplied the rank and file for the new
mass labour movement that unfolded itself in the early
sixties.   One need only examine in detail the history of the
First International to notice at once that the majority of

its members and leaders came from the ranks of the skilled workers in both the building and artistic trades.

Along with this revival of the labour movement came the awakening of the old socialist groups. On the first plane one must notice the Proudhonists. Proudhon was still alive. He had at one time been imprisoned; then he migrated to Belgium where he exerted a certain influence on the labour movement directly as well as through his followers. But the ideas which he now preached differed somewhat from the ideas he had held at the time of his polemics with Marx.

Now it was an altogether peaceful theory adapted to the legalised labour movement. The Proudhonists aimed at a general betterment of the workers' lot and the means offered were to be adapted chiefly to the conditions of the skilled workers. Their chief aim was the reduction of credit rates, or the establishment of free credit, if possible. They recommended the organising of credit associations for the purpose of mutual aid; hence the name Mutualists. Mutual aid societies, no strikes of any sort, the legalisation of workers' societies, free credit, no participation in any immediate political struggles, a desire to better one's lot by using only the economic struggle as the weapon (moreover, this weapon was not to be considered as directed against the foundations of capitalist society)—this, in brief, was the programme of the Mutualists of that day, who in several instances were more moderate than their teacher.

Alongside of this group we find an even more conservative group, who tried to buy the workers by means of sops. Armand Levi, the journalist, who had once been closely connected with the Polish political emigrants was the leader. He was in close relation with the same Prince Plon-Plon whom we already know as the patron of Herr Vogt.

The third—the least numerous, but made up of revolutionists—was the group of Blanquists who had by then resumed their work among the workers as well as among the intelligentsia and the student youth. Among these were Paul Lafargue (1811-1877), and Charles Longuet, both of whom subsequently became Marx's sons-in-law.

Here was also the now famous Georges Clémenceau.* All these young people and workers were under the strong influence of Blanqui. The latter, though in prison, kept up a lively intercourse with the outside world; he had frequent interviews with representatives of these youths. The Blanquists were most implacable foes of the Napoleonic Empire, and impassioned underground revolutionists.

Such was the state of the working-class movement in England and in France in 1862. A series of events then took place which brought about a closer rapprochement between the French and the English workers. Outwardly, the arrangement of the world exposition in London served as the occasion for this rapprochement. This international exposition was the result of the new stage in capitalist production—giant industries which tended to knit separate countries into living parts of world economy. The first exposition was arranged after the February Revolution. It took place in London in 1851; the second, in Paris in 1855; the third, again in London.

In connection with this exposition, there was started in Paris serious agitation among the workers. The group which was headed by Armand Levi turned to Prince Plon-Plon, who was the chairman of the commission which was to organise the French department at the London exposition. The Prince kindly arranged for the granting of subsidies to a delegation of workers which was to be sent to the London exposition.

Bitter controversies arose among the Paris workers. The Blanquists, of course, insisted on rejecting this government favour. Another group in which the Mutualists were preponderant, entertained a different opinion. According to them it was necessary to utilise all legal possibilities. Money was to be given to subsidise a workers' delegation. They demanded that the delegation instead of being appointed from above, should be elected in the workshops. They proposed to utilise these elections for propaganda purposes and for the pressing of their own candidates.

The second group was finally victorious. Elections were permitted, and the delegation was chosen almost entirely from among the members of this group. The Blanquists boycotted the elections. The followers of Armand Levi were completely swamped. Thus was the workingmen's delegation from Paris organised. It is significant that the German delegation to London was connected with that group of workers who were active with Lassalle in the organisation of a labour congress.

In this manner the world exposition at London created an opportunity for the French, English and German workers to come together. Some historians of the International trace its beginning to this meeting. Here is what Steklov writes of it:

"The occasion for the rapprochement and the agreement between the English and the Continental workers was the world's exposition of 1862 in London. On August 5, 1862, the English workers staged a reception in honour of the seventy French delegates. The dominant note in the speeches was the necessity of establishing international ties among the proletarians who as men, as citizens and as toilers had identical interests and aspirations."

Unfortunately, this is mere legend. As a matter of fact this meeting bore an entirely different character. It took place with the participation and approval of the representatives of the bourgeoisie and the ruling classes. The speeches delivered there offended not even one employer, disturbed not even one policeman. Those of the English capitalists who had been at the head of the contractors during the strikes in the building trades were the very ones who took an active part in this meeting. Suffice it to say that the English trade unionists demonstratively refused to take part in this affair. This meeting can under no circumstances be regarded as the origin of the International.

Only one thing was true: In London, the French and German delegations were likely to meet French and German workers who had emigrated after 1848. The place where workers of various nationalities would meet in the fifties and the sixties was the well-known Workers' Educational Society, which had been founded by Schapper and his friends in 1840. The tea-room and the dining-room of this society were situated on a street where foreigners settled; it served as such a centre up to the late war. The English government hastened to close this club immediately upon the declaration of war in 1914.

It was there, no doubt, that some members of the French delegation became acquainted with the old French emigrants, and that the German workers from Leipzig and Berlin met their old comrades. But these were of course only accidental ties which were as unlikely to lead to the forming of the International as was the meeting of August 5, to which Steklov, together with other historians, attaches such great importance.

But now two very important events happened, the first of which was the American Civil War (1860-1865). We have already seen that the abolition of slavery was the most important problem of the day. It became so acute and it had led to such an acrid conflict between the southern and the northern States, that the South, in order to preserve slavery, determined to secede and to organise an independent republic. The result was a war which brought in its train unexpected and unpleasant consequences to the whole of the capitalistic world. The southern States were then the sole growers of the cotton which was used in all the cotton industries of the world. Egyptian cotton was still of very little importance; East India and Turkestan were not producing any cotton at all. Europe thus found itself without any cotton supply. The textile industries of the world were experiencing a crisis. The shortage of cotton caused a rise in the prices of all the other raw materials in the textile industry. Of course, the big capitalists suffered, least of all; the petty capitalists hastened to shut down their factories. Tens, nay hundreds of thousands of workers were doomed to perish of hunger.

The governments confined themselves to handing out pitiful pittances. The English workers who had not long before, during the strike in the building trades, shown an example of solidarity, now too, took up the cause of organising help. The initiative belonged to the London Trades Council, which appointed a special committee. In France also there was organised a special committee for this purpose. The two committees were in frequent communication with one another. It was this that suggested to the French and English workers how closely allied were the interests of labour of different countries. The Civil War in the United States gave a terrific shock to the entire economic life of Europe; its malignant effects were equally felt by the English, French, German, and even Russian workers. This was why Marx wrote in his introduction to *Capital,* that the American Civil War in the nineteenth century, played the same rôle with regard to the working class, as the American War for Independence in the eighteenth century had played with regard to the French bourgeoisie and the French Revolution.

Another event then occurred which also was of equal interest to the workers of the different countries. Serfdom was abolished in Russia (1861). Reforms in other branches of the political and economic life of Russia were imminent. The revolutionary movement became more animated; it advocated more radical changes. Russia's outlying posses-

sions, chiefly Poland, were in a state of commotion.
The Tsar's government grasped at this as the best pretext
for getting rid of external as well internal sedition. It provoked the Polish revolt, while at the same time, aided by
Katkov and other venal scribes, it incited Russian chauvin-
ism at home. The notorious hangman, Muraviev, and other
brutes like him, were commandeered to stifle the Polish
revolt.

In western Europe, where hatred for Russian Czarism
was prevalent, the rebellious Poles evoked the warmest sympathy. The English and French governments allowed the
sympathisers of the Polish insurgents complete freedom of
action, regarding this as a convenient outlet for the stored-
up feelings of resentment. In France a number of meetings
were held, and a committee, headed by Henri Tolain (1828-
1897), and Perruchon, was organised. In England the pro-
Polish movement was headed by the workers, Odger and
Cremer, and by the radical intellectual, Professor Beesly.

In April, 1863, a monster mass meeting was called in
London. Professor E. S. Beesly (1831-1915), presided;[*]
Cremer delivered a speech in defence of the Poles. The
meeting passed a resolution which urged the English and
the French workers to bring simultaneous pressure to bear
upon their respective governments and to force their intervention in favour of the Poles. It was decided to provide
for an International meeting. This took place in London
on July 22, 1863. The chairman was again Beesly. Odger
and Cremer spoke in the name of the English workers;
Tolain, in the name of the French. Nothing but the Polish
affair was discussed, and they all insisted on the necessity
of restoring independence to Poland. On the next day,
another meeting took place to which the historians of the
International have not paid much attention. It was arranged on the initiative of the London Trades Council, this
time without the participation of the bourgeoisie. Odger

had been advocating closer ties between English and Continental labour. The problem presented itself on a practical basis. English labour had to take note of the serious competition of the French, the Belgian, and particularly the German workers. At the beginning of the sixties, the breadbaking industry which was already concentrated into great enterprises was wholly operated by German workers. In the building, furniture, and decorative industries there was an influx of Frenchmen. That was why the English trade unionists valued so much any possible chance of influencing foreign labourers who were pouring into England. This could best be accomplished through an organisation which would unite the workers of various nations.

It was decided that the English workers send an appropriate address to the French workers. Almost three months elapsed, while the draft of this address was being offered to the London trade unionists for approval. It was written largely by Odger.

By this time the Polish revolt had been crushed by the Tsar's henchmen with unheard-of cruelty. The address made almost no mention of it. Here is a small excerpt:

"A fraternity of peoples is highly necessary for the cause of labour, for we find that whenever we attempt to better our social condition by reducing the hours of toil, or by raising the price of labour, our employers threaten us with bringing over Frenchmen, Germans, Belgians and others to do our work at a reduced rate of wages; and we are sorry to say, that this has been done, though not from any desire on the part of our continental brethren to injure us, but through a want of regular and systematic communication between the industrial classes of all countries. Our aim is to bring up the wages of the ill-paid to as near a level as possible with that of those who are better remunerated, and not to allow our employers to play us off one against the other, and so drag us down to the lowest possible condition, suitable to their avaricious bargaining."

The address was translated into French by Professor
Beesly and was sent to Paris in November, 1863. There it
served as material for propaganda in the workshops. The
French answer was very tardy. Paris was then getting
ready for the forthcoming elections to the legislative assembly, later known as the Chamber of Deputies. A group
of workers at the head of whom we again see Tolain and
Perruchon, raised the exceedingly important question as to
whether labour should nominate its own candidates or
whether it should be satisfied to support the radical candidates. In other words, should labour stand on its own independent platform, or should it straggle at the tail of the
bourgeois parties. This question was hectically discussed
at the end of 1863 and in the beginning of 1864. The
workers decided to work independently, and to nominate
Tolain. They resolved to explain this break with the bourgeois democrats in a special platform, which has since been
known as the *Manifesto of the Sixty*, because of the number
of signatures affixed to the document.

The theoretical part of this Manifesto, the criticism to
which the bourgeois order was subjected, was in full accord
with Proudhon's views. But at the same time it definitely
abandoned the master's political programme by advocating
a separate political party for the workers, and the nomina-
tion of labour candidates for political office to represent the
interests of the workers.

Proudhon greeted this *Manifesto of the Sixty* very
warmly. Inspired by it, he proceeded to write a book
which turned out to be the best work he had ever written.
He devoted the last months of his life to it, but he did not
live to see it published. The book was called *The Political
Capacity of the Working Class*. Here for the first time
Proudhon acknowledged the right of the working class to
form independent class organisations. He hailed the new
programme of the Paris workers as the best proof of the

vast political potentialities stored away in the depths of the working class. Despite the fact that Proudhon did not change his stand on the question of strikes and mutual aid associations, his last book, by its spirit of protest against bourgeois society and its decidedly proletarian slant, was reminiscent of his excellent first literary work, *What Is Property?* This justification of the working class became one of the favourite books of the French workers. When we are told of the influence of Proudhonism during the epoch of the First International, we must not forget that it was the influence of that form of Proudhonism which became crystallised after the publication of the *Manifesto of the Sixty.*

Almost a year passed before the workers of Paris composed their reply to the English address. A special delegation was chosen to take it to London. On September 28, 1864, a meeting to receive the French delegation was held in the famous St. Martin's Hall. Beesly presided. The hall was crowded. First Odger read the address from the English workers. Tolain then read the French reply, a short excerpt of which follows:

"Industrial progress, the division of labour, freedom of trade —these are three factors which should receive our attention today, for they promise to change the very substance of the economic life of society. Compelled by the force of circumstances and the demands of the time, capital is concentrating and organising in mighty financial and industrial combinations. Should we not take some defensive measure, this force, if not counterbalanced in some way, will soon be a despotic power. We, the workers of the world, must unite and erect an insurmountable barrier to the baleful system which would divide humanity into two classes: a host of hungry and brutalised people on one hand, and a clique of fat, overfed mandarins on the other. Let us seek our salvation through solidarity."

The French workers brought with them even the project for such an organisation. A central commission made up of representatives from various countries was established in London. Subcommissions which were to be in constant communication with the central body, and which were to discuss questions proposed by that body, were created in all the chief cities in Europe. The central commission was to summarise the results of these discussions. An international congress was to convene in Belgium, to decide upon the final form of the organisation.

But we might ask where was Marx, what part did he take in all this? No part at all. We see, then, that all the preparations for the historic event which took place on September 28, 1864, the day of the beginning of the First International, were the efforts of the workers themselves. Until now we had no occasion even to mention the name of Marx in connection with this affair. Still on this august occasion Marx was among the invited guests on the platform. How did he happen to be there? A little note found among Marx's miscellaneous papers supplies the answer. It reads:

"Mr. Marx,
Dear Sir:
    The committee who have organised the meeting as announced in the enclosed bill respectfully request the favour of your attendance. The production of this will admit you to the Committee Room where the Committee will meet at half past 7.
    I am, sir,
                          Yours respectfully,
                                (Signed) W. R. Cremer."

The question arises, What prompted Cremer to invite Marx? Why was this invitation not extended to many other emigrants who crowded London at the time and who were closer to the Englishmen or the Frenchmen? Why was he chosen as a member of the committee of the future International Association?

As to this, we can form only guesses. The most plausible seems to be the following: We have already seen the part that the Educational Society of the German workers was playing in London as the central meeting place of workers of various nationalities. It became such a centre to an even greater extent when the English workers themselves came to realise that it was necessary to combine with the Germans in order to counteract the harmful consequences of the competition of workers whom the English employers through their agents were luring into London. Hence the close personal ties which existed between them and the members of the former Communist League—J. G. Eccarius, Friedrich Lessner, Pfänder. The first two were tailors, the third, a painter. They were all taking an active part in the London trade-union movement and were well acquainted with the organisers and the leaders of the London Trades Council. It is not difficult to understand how Odger and Cremer came to know Dr. Marx, who during the affair with Vogt had renewed his relations with the German Workers' Educational Society.

Marx's chief rôle in the First International, with the foundation of which he had nothing to do, began after it was organised. He soon became the guiding spirit of the organisation. The committee that was elected by the meeting of September 28, had no instructions. There was no programme, nor constitution, nor even a name. There was already existing in London such an international society, the Common League, which offered its hospitality to the committee. From a reading of the minutes of the committee's first meeting we gather that there were present also several benign bourgeois representatives of this League. Some of these gentlemen suggested to the committee that there was no need for a new organisation, others proposed the organisation of a new international society which would be open not only to workers but also to anybody to whom the cause of international solidarity and the amelioration of the economic and political conditions of the toilers were dear. Only on the insistence of two workingmen, Eccarius and Whitlock, a former Chartist, was it decided to christen the new society with the name of International Workingmen's Association. This motion·was supported by the Englishmen, among whom there were a few Chartists, members of the old Workingmen's Association, the cradle of the Chartist movement.

The new name unequivocally defined the distinctive character of the new international association which forthwith shook off the well-meaning bourgeoisie, who belonged to the Common League. The committee was told to look for other quarters. Fortunately, they were successful in finding a small meeting room not far from the German Workers' Educational Society, in a district populated by emigrants and foreign workers.

As soon as the name was decided upon, the committee proceeded to compose the programme and the statutes. There was one trouble; the committee was made up of too many different elements. There were first of all Englishmen, who were divided up into several groups themselves. There were trade unionists, former Chartists; there were even ex-Owenites. There were Frenchmen, not very great adepts at economic questions, but who considered themselves specialists along the lines of revolution. The Italians, too, were very influential for they were headed by Giuseppe Mazzini (1805-1872), the very popular old revolutionist, republican, but who was also very religious. There were also the Polish emigrants. To them the Polish question was paramount. There were, finally, several Germans, all former members of the Communist League—Eccarius, Lessner, Lochner, Pfänder and Marx.

Various projects were brought before the committee. In the subcommittee on which he was serving, Marx propounded his theses and it was finally resolved that he present his project before the whole committee. Finally, when the committee convened for the fourth time (November 1, 1864), Marx's draft with a small number of editorial modifications was adopted by an overwhelming majority.

We must admit at the very outset that the draft, as it was adopted, contained many compromises and concessions. Marx himself, in his letter to Engels, deplores the fact that he was forced to introduce into the constitution and the programme such words as Right, Morality and Justice, but, as he assures Engels, he managed to insert these words in places where they would do least harm.

Yet this was not what contained the secret of Marx's success. His success in having his propositions adopted almost unanimously by such a variegated group was the result of the extraordinary mastery with which the Inaugural Address of the International was written. This was admitted even by Bakunin, Marx's most virulent opponent. As Marx confesses in his letter to Engels, it was extremely difficult to couch the communist view in a form that would prove acceptable to the labour movement in its first crude stages. It was impossible to employ the bold revolutionary language of the *Communist Manifesto*. Marx endeavoured to be sweeping in content yet moderate in form. His success was unequivocal.

This Inaugural Address was written seventeen years after the *Communist Manifesto*. These two documents were the work of the same author. Yet the historical epochs in which, and the organisations for which, these two manifestoes were written, were utterly different. The *Communist Manifesto* was written at the request of a small group of revolutionists and communists for a very young labour movement. These communists emphasised even then that they were not stressing any principles which they wanted to foist upon the labour movement, but that they were trying to crystallise those general principles which, irrespective of nationality, represented the common interests of the proletariat of the entire world.

In 1864 the labour movement grew, and penetrated the masses. But as far as a developed class consciousness was concerned it was much behind the revolutionary vanguard of 1848. A similar retrogression was also to be observed among the leaders. The new Manifesto had to be written in a manner which would take into account the low level of proletarian class consciousness among the masses and the leaders, but which would at the same time adhere to the basic principles laid down in the *Communist Manifesto*.

Marx, in the Address, gave a classical example of "united front" tactics. He formulated the demands and emphasised all the points upon which the working class could and should unite, and on the basis of which a further development of the labour movement could be expected. From the immediate proletarian demands formulated by Marx the greater demands of the *Communist Manifesto* would logically follow.

In all this Marx had, of course, a colossal advantage over Mazzini, over the French revolutionists, as well as over the English socialists who were on the committee of the International. He himself, without having changed his basic principles, accomplished a monumental piece of work. By this time he had concluded the first draft of his gigantic work and was engaged in putting his finishing touches to the first volume of *Capital*. Marx was then the only man in the world who had made such an exhaustive study of the conditions of the working class and had so profoundly grasped the whole mechanism of capitalist society. In the whole of England there was not another man who took the infinite pains of making such a thorough study of all the reports of the English factory inspectors and the researches of the parliamentary commissions which had been investigating conditions in various branches of industry and different categories of the city and the country proletariat. The information which Marx possessed on this subject was comprehensive and incomparably wider than that possessed by the workingmen-members of the committee. He knew conditions in each trade and their relation to the general laws of capitalist production.

The gifts of a great propagandist are shown in the very structure of the Address. Just as in the *Communist Manifesto*, Marx began with the class struggle as the fundamental basis of all historic development and of all political movements, so did he in the new Manifesto begin not with general phrases, nor with high-flown subjects, but with facts which characterised the conditions of the working class.

"It is an extremely momentous fact that the misery of the working class in the years 1848-1864 has not lessened, in spite of the unexampled development of industry and growth of trade during this period."

And Marx referring to Gladstone's speech in the House of Commons pointed out that despite the three-fold increase of the trade of Great Britain since 1843, human life in nine cases out of ten was nothing but a hard struggle for a mere existence. In fact, criminals in prison were getting better nourishment than many workers.

Constantly referring to the investigations of the parliamentary commissions, Marx drew a picture of undernourishment, degeneration, and disease among the masses of the working class. At the same time he called attention to the fabulous growth of the wealth of the propertied classes.

Marx thus arrived at the inevitable conclusion that, notwithstanding the assertions of the bourgeois economists, neither the perfecting of the machine, nor the application of science to industry, nor the opening of new means of communication, the discovery of new colonies, emigration, the creation of new markets, nor free trade were likely to eliminate

the misery of the working class.   He therefore concluded
further, as in the *Communist Manifesto*, that while the social
order rested on the old foundation, any new development of
the productive powers of labour would only widen and deepen
the chasm which divided the classes and would bring to the
fore even more strikingly the already existing antagonism.

Having pointed out the causes which had contributed to
the defeat of the working class in 1848, the defeat which
had brought in its train the apathy that had characterised
the decade from 1849 to 1859, Marx also directed attention
to a few conquests made by the workers during that period.

First, the ten-hour day law.   He proved that, despite all
the assertions of the hangers-on of capitalism, the shortening
of the workday enhanced, rather than impaired, the produc-
tivity of labour.   Moreover, Marx pointed out the triumph of
the principle of government interference in economic relations
over the old *laissez-faire* ideas.   He further concluded, as
he had in the *Communist Manifesto*, that production must
be subjected to the control and the direction of society
as a whole, and that such social production lay at the very
basis of the political economy of the working class.   The
law pertaining to the ten-hour day was not merely a practical victory, it indicated the victory of proletarian political
economy over the political economy of the bourgeoisie.

Another achievement was the co-operative factories which
were being built on the initiative of the workers themselves.
But, unlike Lassalle for whom co-operative associations were
the starting point of the transformation of society into a
state of socialism, Marx did not exaggerate their practical
importance.   On the contrary, he used these co-operatives
to illustrate to the working masses that large scale and
scientific production could proceed and develop without a
class of capitalists to exploit the toilers; that wage labour,
like slavery, was not anything eternal, but that, in point of
fact, it was a transitional and lower form of work which

ultimately was to give place to a system of social production. Having made all the communist deductions, Marx
pointed out that while these co-operative associations comprised only a small number of workers, they could not better
the conditions of the working class in any way.

The network of co-operative production would have to
spread all over the land before capitalist production could
be superseded by communist production. But having put
the problem thus wise, Marx hastened to note that such a
transformation would be impeded by the desperate opposition of the ruling classes. The landowners and the capitalists would use their political power to defend their
economic privileges. Hence, the first duty of the working
class was the conquest of political power, and, to accomplish
this, the workers must create political labour parties in all
the countries of the world. There is only one factor of success that the workers have at their command. This is mass,
numbers. But this mass is strong only when it is compact,
united, and when it is guided by knowledge and science.
Without compactness, without solidarity, without mutual
support in the struggle for liberation, without a national
and an international organisation the workers would be
doomed to failure. Guided by these considerations, added
Marx, the workers of various countries decided to form an
International Workingmen's Association.

Thus did Marx with his amazing tact and skill again
arrive at the basic conclusions he had once reached in the
more fiery *Communist Manifesto*: the organisation of the
proletariat along class lines, the overthrow of bourgeois
domination, the proletarian seizure of political power, the
abolition of wage labour, the passing of all the means of
production into the hands of society.

Marx concluded the Inaugural Address with another quite
important political problem. The working class must not
confine itself to the narrow sphere of national politics. It

must follow assiduously all the questions of external politics. If the success of the whole cause depends upon the fraternal solidarity of the workers of the world, then the working class would not fulfill its mission, were it to allow the ruling classes who are in charge of international diplomacy to utilise national prejudices, to set the workers of one country against the workers of other countries to shed the blood and destroy the wealth of the people. The workers must therefore master all the mysteries of international politics. They must watch the diplomatic acts of their governments; they must resist, if need be with all the power at their disposal; they must join in one sweeping protest against the criminal machinations of their governments. It is time to bring to an end a state of affairs which, while punishing crimes when perpetrated by individuals, permits stealing, robbing and deceit in international relations.

CHAPTER VIII

WE have covered in detail the history of the foundation
of the International and the writing of its Inaugural Address. We shall now proceed to study the Constitution of
the International. It, too, was written by Marx and was
composed of two parts; one a statement of principles, the
other dealing with organisation problems.

We have seen how skillfully Marx introduced the basic
principles of communism into the Inaugural Address of the
International. But still more important and incomparably
more difficult was the introduction of these principles into
the Constitution. The Inaugural Address pursued only one
aim—the elucidation of the motives which impelled the
workers to assemble on September 28, 1864, and to found
the International. But this was not yet a programme, it
was only an introduction to it; it was merely a solemn pro-
nunciamento before the whole world—and this was particularly brought out in its very name—that a new international
association, an association of workers, was being founded.

In not a less masterly fashion did Marx succeed in solving
the second problem—the formulation of the general problems confronting the working class in different countries.

"Considering,
"That the emancipation of the working classes must be conquered by the working classes themselves; that the struggle for

155

the emancipation of the working classes means not a struggle for class privileges and monopolies, but for equal rights and duties, and the abolition of all class rule;

"That the economical subjection of the man of labour to the monopoliser of the means of labour, that is, the sources of life, lies at the bottom of servitude in all its forms, of all social misery, mental degradation, and political dependence;

"That the economical emancipation of the working classes is therefore the great end to which every political movement ought to be subordinate as a means;

"That all efforts aiming at that great end have hitherto failed from the want of solidarity between the manifold divisions of labour in each country, and from the absence of a fraternal bond of union between the working classes of different countries;

"That the emancipation of labour is neither a local nor a national, but a social problem, embracing all countries in which modern society exists, and depending for its solution on the concurrence, practical and theoretical, of the most advanced countries;

"That the present revival of the working classes in the most industrious countries of Europe, while it raises a new hope, gives solemn warning against a relapse into the old errors, and calls for the immediate combination of the still disconnected movements."

A careful perusal of these points reveals how closely the Communist Party of Russia had, in some planks of its programme, followed the theses formulated by Marx. The same is true of the old programmes of the English, French, and German parties. In the French and the Erfurt programmes [1] particularly, there are many points that are actually a literal transcription of the basic premises of the Constitution of the First International.

Of course, not all the members of the provisional committee of the International understood these propositions in the same way. For instance, the English, French, and German members all agreed on the proposition that the emancipation

[1] The programme adopted at the Erfurt Congress (1891) of the German Social-Democratic Party.

of the working class could be achieved only by the working class itself; but this was interpreted differently by each group. The English trade unionists and the ex-Chartists saw in this proposition a protest against the irksome solicitude bestowed upon the workers by the benign members of the middle class. The Frenchmen, who were strongly incensed against the intelligentsia, understood this proposition in the sense of a warning against the treacherous intelligentsia and an affirmation of the ability of the working class to get on without it. Only the Germans, the former members of the Communist League, really grasped all the implications of this proposition. If the working class could emancipate itself only through its own efforts, then any coalition with the bourgeoisie, any hobnobbing with the capitalists would be in sharp opposition to this principle. It was also emphasised that the aim was not to emancipate this or that group of workers, but the working class as a whole, and that the emancipation could be accomplished not by one or another group of workers but by the entire working class, and that this would presuppose a class organisation of the proletariat. From the proposition that capitalist monopoly of the means of production is the cause of the economic enslavement of the working class, it followed that it would be necessary to destroy this monopoly. And this deduction was further strengthened by the demand for the abolition of any class rule, which, of course, could not be attained without the abolition of the division of society into classes.

The proposition, stated in the Inaugural Address, was not repeated in the Constitution.[2] In it there was no direct assertion that for the realisation of all the aims the proletariat had put before itself, it was necessary for it to obtain political power. Instead of this, we find another statement. The Constitution maintained "That the economic emancipation of the working classes is therefore the great end to

[2] Published as Rules of the International Workingmen's Association.

which every political movement ought to be subordinate as a means."

Since this proposition subsequently became the starting point of most furious disagreements in the First International, we must explain it.

What did this proposition imply? The great goal of the proletarian movement was the economic liberation of the working class. This goal could be reached only by expropriating the monopolists of the means of production, by the abolition of all class rule. But how could this be accomplished? Were the "pure" socialists and anarchists right in their deprecation of political struggle?

No, was the reply contained in the thesis formulated by Marx. The struggle of the working class on the political field is as necessary as it is on the economic field. Political organisation is necessary. The political movement of the proletariat must needs develop. It must not however be regarded, as it is regarded by the bourgeois democrats and the radical intelligentsia, as something independent. These are only interested in the change of political forms, in the establishment of a republic; they want to hear nothing of the fundamental questions. This was why Marx emphasised that for the proletariat, the political movement was only a means for the attainment of their great ends, that it was a subsidiary movement. This statement was, to be sure, not as clear cut as the one given in the *Communist Manifesto* or even in the Inaugural Address, where it was expressly stated that the cardinal aim of the working class was to gain political power.

True, to the English members of the International the proposition as it was formulated by Marx was quite clear. The Constitution was written in the English language, and Marx utilised the terms with which the former Chartists and Owenites, who were members of the committee, were thoroughly familiar. Apropos of this we should recall that the

Chartists' quarrel with the Owenites had been chiefly on the ground that the latter took cognizance only of the "great end" and insisted on ignoring the political struggle. When the Chartists advanced the Charter with its famous six points, the Owenites accused them of having forgotten socialism completely. Then the Chartists on their part asserted that for them, too, the political struggle was not the chief aim. Thus twenty years before, the Chartists had formulated the proposition which was now repeated by Marx. For them, the Chartists maintained, the political struggle is a means to an end, not an end in itself. We can see then why Marx's thesis did not arouse any opposition in the committee. Only a few years later, when the heated discussions between the Bakuninists and their opponents arose, did this point become the bone of contention. The Bakuninists maintained that originally the words "as a means" were not contained in the Constitution and that Marx purposely smuggled them in later to foist his conception of politics on the International. An omission of the words "as a means" does no doubt change the whole meaning of this point. In the French translation of the Constitution these words were actually omitted.

A little misunderstanding arose which could have been easily explained but which in the heat of factional conflict led to the absurd accusation against Marx of falsification, of forging the Constitution of the International. When the Constitution had been translated the French official edition did not contain the words "as a means." The French text reads: "The economic emancipation of the working class is the great end, to which the political movement ought to be subordinate." This was deemed necessary in order not to attract the attention of Bonaparte's police which regarded with great suspicion any political movement among the workers. At the beginning the police did actually consider the French Internationalists as interested more in economics than in politics. Precisely on the same grounds did the Blanquists who were "politicians," also attack the poor internationalists as "economists."

The trouble was still more aggravated by the fact that this incorrect French translation of the Constitution was reprinted in the French part of Switzerland and from there it was spread through all the countries where the French language was most familiar—Italy, Spain, and Belgium. We shall see later, that at the first general congress, which ratified the temporary Constitution of the International, each nation accepted the text which it had before it. The First International was too poor to print its Constitution in three languages. Even the English text was printed only in a thousand copies, all of which were soon gone. Guillaume, one of the most bitter opponents of Marx, and the one who most persistently accused Marx of forgery, assures us in his *History of the International* that only in 1905 did he see for the first time the English text with the words "as a means" included! Had he wanted to, he could have convinced himself long before that Marx was not a falsifier, but this would not materially have changed the course of events. We know full well that on the question of tactics the most violent discords may arise when to all appearances the conflicting parties adhere in principle to the same programme.

The Constitution contained another point against which, it is true, the anarchists did not protest but which from the point of view of Marxism inspires doubts. We have already mentioned that, in order to reach an agreement among the highly diversified elements which entered into the make-up of the committee, Marx was forced to compromise on some points. These were made not in the Inaugural Address, but in the Constitution. We shall soon see what these compromises were.

Right after the presentation of the principles, on the basis of which the members of the committee that was elected at the meeting of September 28, 1864, had decided to found the International Workingmen's Association, Marx continued:

"The first International Working Men's Congress declares that this International Association and all societies and individuals adhering to it will acknowledge truth, justice, and morality, as the basis of their conduct towards each other, and towards all men, without regard to colour, creed or nationality;

"This Congress considers it the duty of a man to claim the rights of a man and a citizen, not only for himself but for every man who does his duty, No rights without duties, no duties without rights."

Wherein lay the concessions made by Marx? We observe that concerning this he himself wrote to Engels, "All my suggestions were adopted by the subcommittee. I was compelled to insert into the Constitution some phrases about 'rights' and 'duties,' as well as 'truth, morality, and justice' but all this is so placed that it is not likely to bring any harm."

And it really was not anything catastrophic. There is nothing terrible, *per se*, in the words Truth, Justice, and Morality, as long as we realise that these concepts are not eternal, unalterable, and independent of social conditions. Marxism does not deny truth, justice, and morality; it merely proves that the evolution of these concepts is determined by historical developments, and that different social classes see in them different contents.

It would have been bad had Marx been compelled to reiterate the declaration of the French and English socialists, had he been forced to say that we must fight for socialism in the name of truth, justice and morality and not because, as he had so marvellously presented in the Inaugural Address, it is inevitable, because it logically follows from the very condition created by capitalism and from the very situation of the working class. As these words were put in by Marx they merely stated that the members of the International Workingmen's Association were obliged to conduct themselves in their relations to each other in the spirit of truth, justice, and morality, that is, not to betray each other or the class to which they belonged, not to deceive each other, to act in a comradely spirit, etc. Instead of the principles upon which the Utopian Socialists had based their demand for socialism, these concepts were now transmuted by Marx into basic rules of conduct within the proletarian organisation itself.

But the point which we are now discussing declares that these principles must serve as a basis for the conduct of the members of the International in their relation to all persons regardless of race, religion, or nationality. And this was not less useful. We must bear in mind that at this time in the United States there raged the Civil War; that shortly before the Polish insurrection had been definitely crushed; that the Czar's armies were bringing to a successful conclusion the conquest of the Caucasus; that religious persecution was still going on throughout most of the civilised countries; that even in England the Jews were given political rights only toward the end of the fifties, and that not only in Russia but in other European states, too, they were not yet enjoying full civil rights.

The bourgeoisie had not yet materialised the "eternal" principles of morality and justice even where members of their own class in their own countries were involved. These principles were most unceremoniously trampled upon where members of other countries or nationalities were concerned.

The point pertaining to Rights and Duties was much more objectionable. There was neither rime nor reason for urging each member to fight for his rights as a man and as a citizen; to fight not only for himself but for others. Here Marx, despite his great diplomatic skill, was forced to make a serious concession to the representatives of the French revolutionary emigrants who were on the committee.

Let us recall now some facts concerning the Great French Revolution. One of the first acts was the declaration of the rights of man and of the rights of citizenship. In its struggle against the landed aristocracy and absolutism which was appropriating all the privileges and was imposing on others all the duties, the revolutionary bourgeoisie brought forward demands for equality, fraternity, and liberty, and demands that every man, every citizen, should be recognised as possessing a number of inalienable rights. Among these the sacred irrefragable right of private property was particularly stressed. This right was being unhesitatingly violated by the aristocracy and by the royal power where the property of the Third Estate was concerned.

The Jacobins introduced only a few corrections into this declaration of rights. The point concerning the sacredness of private property was left intact. The declaration was rendered more radical with respect to politics, for it sanctioned the right of the people to revolt and it emphasised the brotherhood of all nations. In this form it is known as the Declaration of Rights of 1793 or of Robespierre, and it became the programme of the French revolutionists from the beginning of 1830.

On the other hand Mazzini's adherents insisted on the acceptance of his programme.* In his famous book, *On the Duties of Man,* which was translated into English and which won wide popularity there among the workers, Mazzini, in accord with his slogan, "God and the People," and in contradistinction to the French materialists with their declaration of the rights of man based on reason and nature, advanced the conception of duty, of obligations, instilled by God in man as the fundamental premise of his idealistic ethics.

We now understand the derivation of Marx's formula: There are no rights without duties, there are no duties without rights.   Forced to incorporate the demands from the Declaration of Rights, Marx utilized the controversy between the Frenchmen and the Italians to underline in his formulation the distinction between this demand and the former demand of the bourgeoisie.   The proletariat also demands its rights but it declares at the outset that it does not admit the rights of the individual without the individual's corresponding duties to society.

When a few years later, the Constitution was re-examined, Marx suggested that only the words referring to the Declaration of Rights be stricken out.   The proposition dealing with Rights and Duties was retained, and was later incorporated into the Erfurt Programme in the form of Equal Rights and Equal Duties.

We shall now pass on to the study of the Constitution itself.

"1. This Association is established to afford a central medium of communication and co-operation between Working Men's Societies existing in different countries and aiming at the same end; viz., the protection, advancement, and complete emancipation of the working classes.

"2. The name of the Society shall be The International Working Men's Association.

"3. There shall annually meet a General Working Men's Congress, consisting of delegates of the branches of the Association.   The Congress will have to proclaim the common aspirations of the working class, take the measures required for the successful working of the International Association, and appoint the General Council of the Society.

"4. Each Congress appoints the time and place of meeting for the next Congress.   The delegates assemble at the appointed time and place without any special invitation.   The General Council may, in case of need, change the place, but has no power to postpone the time of meeting.   The Congress appoints the seat and elects the members of the General Council annually. The General Council thus elected shall have power to add to the number of its members.

"On its annual meetings, the General Congress shall receive a public account of the annual transactions of the General Council. The latter may, in cases of emergency, convoke the General Congress before the regular yearly term.

"5. The General Council shall consist of working men from the different countries represented in the International Association. It shall from its own members elect the officers necessary for the transaction of business, such as a treasurer, a general secretary, corresponding secretaries for the different countries, etc.

"6. The General Council shall form an international agency between the different national and local groups of the Association, so that the working men in one country be constantly informed of the movements of their class in every other country; that an inquiry into the social state of the different countries of Europe be made simultaneously, and under a common direction; that the questions of general interest mooted in one society be ventilated by all; and that when immediate practical steps should be needed—as, for instance, in case of international quarrels—the action of the associated societies be simultaneous and uniform. Whenever it seems opportune, the General Council shall take the initiative of proposals to be laid before the different national or local societies. To facilitate the communications, the General Council shall publish periodical reports.

"7. Since the success of the working men's movement in each country cannot be secured but by the power of union and combination, while, on the other hand, the usefulness of the International General Council must greatly depend on the circumstance whether it has to deal with a few national centres of working men's associations, or with a great number of small and disconnected local societies; the members of the International Association shall use their utmost efforts to combine the disconnected working men's societies of their respective countries into national bodies, represented by central national organs."

The basic principles of this Constitution were later ratified by the Congress. One of the essential changes introduced on Marx's initiative was the abolition of the office of the President of the Central, or as it was later called, the General Council. The experience of the General German Labour Union which had been organised by Lassalle showed all the inconveniences bound up with this utterly useless institution. For conducting its meetings the General Council now elected a chairman. The current affairs were taken care of by a meeting of secretaries from the various national organisations in co-operation with a general secretary.

The Constitution of the International has been utilised more than once in the history of the international labour movement. The scope of this work does not allow a more detailed study of the various changes that were introduced into it during its eight years. In its main features it remained unchanged. Towards the end of the First International, more power was delegated to the General Council.

The all-absorbing problem of the temporary Council was the calling together of an International Congress. This was the cause of heated discussions. Marx maintained that all the preliminary work be completed first so that the different countries should first have the opportunity of acquainting themselves with the problems confronting the International and of organising a bit. The Englishmen, on the contrary, putting the interests of their trade-union movement above everything else, demanded the immediate convocation of a Congress. The French emigrants in the Central Council were allied with them.

The whole affair terminated in a compromise. In 1865 there was convened not a congress but a conference. It took place in London and it was chiefly preoccupied with the examination of reports and the arranging of the order of business for the next congress. Switzerland, England, Belgium, and France were represented. Things did not look very promising. It was decided to call a congress for May, 1866.

In Germany, despite the existence of the General Labour Union, affairs were in an even worse state. Lassalle was killed in a duel on August 30, 1864. In accordance with the constitution of the Union, Bernhard Becker, a man of small capabilities and little influence, became president. A much greater influence was wielded by J. B. Schweitzer (1833-1875), the editor of the central organ of the Union, *The Social-Democrat*. Very soon, however, serious disagreements on questions of internal politics arose between him and Wilhelm Liebknecht who had shortly before become a member of the editorial staff. Marx and Engels who had agreed to contribute to the paper, were soon driven publicly to disclaim all connections with it. The late Mehring attempted to defend Schweitzer; he asserted that in this case Marx and Engels had been wrong. But Mehring was in error. All the facts speak against him.

We have already seen that there had been serious flaws in Lassalle's tactics, that he had allowed himself inadmissible stratagems with respect to the ruling clique. Schweitzer went even further. He printed a series of articles which, Mehring himself admits, created a very unpleasant impression by their sycophantic cringing before Bismarck. Mehring endeavoured to justify it, claiming that such methods were needed in view of the prevailing legal conditions. Liebknecht, the veteran revolutionist, could not, it was claimed, adapt himself and so he set his old friends and teachers upon Schweitzer. Schweitzer and Liebknecht separated. The latter was supported by Marx and Engels, and even by their old opponents, such as Hess, who, too, could not reconcile themselves with Schweitzer's methods. The old revolutionists nicknamed Schweitzer's party "Bismarck's Party."

When the London conference met, Marx's friends in Germany had neither a publication nor real organisation. The Lassalleans refused to have anything to do with the International. As a result of the schism, the Germans were represented in the International only by the old German emigrants who were then domiciled in England and Switzerland.

At the London conference it became clear that the finances of the International were in a most deplorable state. It appeared that for a whole year only about one hundred and fifty dollars were collected. The whole turnover amounted to about thirty-three pounds sterling. With such an income it was difficult to carry on activity on a large scale. It was hardly enough for meeting the most necessary expenses.

During the discussions of the order of business, other disagreements came to light, that arose between the Frenchmen who lived in London and the Frenchmen who represented the Paris organisation. The latter were against taking up the question of Polish independence for they regarded it as purely political. On their part, the French emigrants, supported by some Englishmen, demanded that the question of religion be placed on the order of the day; they clamoured for an unflinching war upon religious prejudice. Marx declared himself against this. He based his opposition on the sound belief that in view of the still weak ties that were holding the labour movement of the different countries together, the injection of the religious question would generate unnecessary friction. He, however, remained in the minority.

Another year elapsed before the first Congress was called. During the interval there occurred a number of important events. In England this was a year of intensive political conflict. The English trade unions, led by the workers who were members of the General Council, were carrying on a stubborn struggle for a wider suffrage. This struggle, we repeat, was developing under the direction of the International. Marx tried his utmost to prevent the English workers from repeating their old mistakes. He wanted them to fight independently without entering into entangling alliances with the radicals. But in the beginning of 1866 the old tendency manifested itself—the tendency that had caused such harm to the English labour movement during the era of Chartism, and that is still having its deleterious effects on it. Since universal suffrage was the object, the proletarian leaders, partly because of financial considerations, entered into an agreement with the most radical section of the bourgeois democracy which had universal suffrage on their programme. To conduct this fight a joint committee was organised, made up of the most variegated elements. Here, there were such highly respectable democrats as Professor Beesly; here, too, were representatives of the so-called free professions—lawyers, judges, representatives of the petty, the middle, and particularly the commercial bourgeoisie who, from the very beginning were inclining toward compromise. The struggle was carried on in the English manner. Meetings and demonstrations were arranged. In July, 1866, London witnessed a demonstration, the size of which it had not seen even in the time of Chartism. The government was finally convinced that concessions were unavoidable.

We shall now recall that after the July Revolution of 1830 a strong movement for parliamentary reforms had taken place in England. It had all culminated in a compromise, the workers were cheated in the most unpardonable fashion, and the right to vote was won only by the industrial bourgeoisie. So it happened now. When the government saw that its retreat was inevitable, and that the city workers were in a threatening mood, it proposed a compromise—the broadening of the suffrage right to include the city proletariat.

We should specify that universal suffrage meant universal male suffrage. The granting of this right to the women was not even thought of. The compromise was immediately accepted by the bourgeois members of the committee of electoral reforms. Suffrage was granted to workers who had a definite abode, even if it consisted of one room, for which they paid a specific minimum rental. Thus the right to vote was won by almost all the urban workers, with the exception of the very indigent ones of whom there were at the time a considerable number in the English cities. The rural proletariat

still remained without the right to vote. This clever trick
was invented by Disraeli, the leader of the English conservatives, and was subscribed to by the bourgeois reformers who
persuaded the workers to accept the concessions with the
view to a further struggle for an extension of the suffrage.
But the rural workers had to wait another twenty years,
while the workers without permanent homes were given suffrage only after the liberalising influence of the Revolution
of 1905 in Russia.

Events not less important took place in Germany in the
years 1865-1866. A furious conflict broke out between
Prussia and Austria. The mooted question was hegemony
within Germany. Bismarck's objective was the final exclusion of Austria from the German Confederation, and the
elevation of Prussia to a dominant place among the remaining German states. This controversy developed into an
armed conflict between Austria and Prussia. In two or three
weeks Prussia, which had no scruples about entering into an
alliance with Italy against another German state, smashed
Austria to pieces and annexed several petty German states
which had been helping Austria—the Kingdom of Hanover,
the free city of Frankfort, the Hesse principality, etc.
Austria was definitely thrown out of the German Confederation. The North-German Confederation headed by Prussia
was organized. To win the sympathies of the workers, Bismarck introduced universal suffrage.

In France, Napoleon was forced to make some concessions.
A few laws dealing with combinations of workers were eliminated from the criminal code. The persecution of economic
organisations, particularly co-operatives and societies for
mutual aid, was weakened. The moderate wing among the
workers, with its emphasis on legal means, was gaining
strength. On the other hand Blanquist organisations were
growing. These fought the Internationalists tooth and nail,

accusing them of abandoning revolutionary action and of coquetting with Bonaparte's government.

In Switzerland, the workers were engaged in their local affairs and only the emigrants from other countries took an interest in the International. The German section, headed by Becker, which published the *Vorbote*, played the rôle of a centre for that portion of the workers in Germany who, unlike the Lassalleans, adhered to the International.

The Congress convened in Geneva in September, 1866, shortly after Prussia had defeated Austria, and the English workers had won what had then appeared to them as a great political victory over the bourgeoisie. The Congress was opened with a scandal. Besides the Proudhonists, there came from France the Blanquists, who also insisted on participating in the work of the Congress. These were mostly students of very revolutionary tendencies. They acted most pertinaciously, although they had no mandate. They were finally quite indecorously thrown out; it was even rumoured that there was an attempt to drown them in the Lake Geneva, but this is a fairy tale. But the dénouement did not come off without the application of fistic and pedal energy, this being the usual thing when Frenchmen are embroiled in a factional fight.

When, however, the work was started, a battle royal occurred between the Proudhonists and the delegation of the General Council which consisted of Eccarius and some English workers. Marx himself could not come, he was busy putting the finishing touches to the first volume of *Capital*. Furthermore, for a sick man who was also under the vigilant surveillance of French and German spies such a journey would have been difficult. But Marx wrote a very detailed report for the delegation concerning all the points to be taken up at the Congress.

The French delegation presented a very painstaking report which was an exposition of the economic ideas of Proudhon. They declared themselves to be vigorously opposed to woman labour, claiming that nature itself designated woman for a place near the family hearth, and that woman's place is in the home and not the factory. Declaring themselves definitely opposed to strikes and to trade unions, they propounded the ideas of co-operation and particularly the organisation of exchange on the principles of mutualism. The first conditions were agreements entered into by separate co-operatives, and the establishment of free credit. They even insisted that the Congress ratify an organisation for international credit, but all they succeeded in doing was to have a resolution adopted which advised all the sections of the International to take up the study of the question of credit and the consolidation of all the workers' loan associations. They even objected to legislative interference with the length of the workday.

They met with the opposition of the English and the German delegates. Point by point they brought forward in the form of resolutions the corresponding parts of Marx's report.

This report insisted that the chief function of the International was the unification and co-ordination of the divers efforts of the working class fighting for its interests. It was necessary to weave such ties so that the labourers of the different countries should not merely feel themselves comrades in battle but that they should also work as members of one army of liberation. It was necessary to organise international aid in cases of strikes and to interfere with the free movement of strikebreakers from one country into another.

As one of the most important problems, Marx stressed scientific research into the conditions of the working class which should be instituted on the initiative of the working class itself. All the collected materials should be directed to the General Council to be worked over. Marx even indicated briefly the chief points of this working-class inquiry.

The question of trade unions provoked most vehement debates. The Frenchmen objected to strikes and to any organised resistance to the employers. The workers must seek their salvation through co-operatives only. The London delegates pressed as a counter-proposal that section of Marx's report which dealt with trade unions. This was adopted by the Congress; but the same misunderstanding occurred here as had with regard to the other regulations of the First International. The exact text was not known for a long time. The Germans knew it through a very unsatisfactory translation published in Becker's *Vorbote;* the French knew it through an even worse translation.

All that had been said by Marx in the *Poverty of Philosophy* and in the *Communist Manifesto* concerning trade unions as the basic nuclei of the class organisation of the proletariat was restated by him in the resolution in a still more definite form. There were also pointed out the contemporary problems of the trade unions and the defects that were typical of them when they were transformed into narrow guild organisations. Let us examine this a little more closely.

How did trade unions originate? How have they developed? They are the result of the struggle between capital and wage labour. In this struggle, the workers find themselves in very unfavourable circumstances. Capital is a social force concentrated and focused in the hands of the capitalists. The worker has only his labour power at his disposal. Thus all talk of a free agreement between the capitalist and the labourer is mere cant and nonsense. When the followers of Proudhon prated of a free and a just agreement, they simply betrayed their ignorance of the mechanism of the capitalist process of production. An agreement between capital and labour can never be concluded on a just basis, even according to the moral standards of a society which places the material means necessary for life and labour on one side and the living productive energy on the other. Behind the individual capitalist there is a social force. The only thing the workers have with which to counteract this force is numbers. But this power of numbers, the mass, is destroyed by a division among the workers, which is created and maintained by the competition for jobs. Thus the first problem that confronted the working class was the elimination of competition. Thus trade unions arose from the voluntary attempts of the workers themselves to set aside, or at least to modify, this competition and to achieve conditions for an agreement which would enable them to rise above the status of mere slaves. Their immediate problem was limited to ordinary needs, to the discovery of ways to stall the ceaseless usurpation of capital, to questions of wages and the number of working hours. Contrary to the assertions of the Proudhonists, this activity is not only thoroughly just, it is also indispensable. It is unavoidable while the present system of production continues to exist. It has to go further, and become more general. And this can only be accomplished through education and international combinations of workers.

But they play another and not less important rôle, which the followers of Proudhon understood as little in 1866 as their teacher had understood it in 1847. Unconsciously, the trade unions served and still serve as points around which workers' organisations were and are crystallised. Their function is reminiscent of the function of the municipalities and the communes in·the development of the bourgeoisie. And if they are indispensable for the guerrilla war between capital and labour, they are even more important as organised factors in the abolition of the very system of wage labour.

Unfortunately, the trade unions have not yet clearly

grasped the full significance of this aspect of their rôle in social evolution. Too exclusively absorbed in their local and immediate struggles with capital, the trade unions have not yet fully realised the force of their activity against the system of wage slavery. This is why they kept and still keep aloof from general and political movements.

Marx pointed out certain signs which indicated that the trade unions were apparently beginning to wake up to some understanding of their historic mission. These signs he saw in the participation of the English trade unions in the struggle for universal suffrage as well as in the resolutions adopted at their conference in Sheffield recommending that all the trade unions join the International.

In conclusion, Marx, who until now was directing his artillery at the followers of Proudhon, addressed himself to the pure-and-simple trade unionists, criticising them for their tendency to limit themselves to questions of wages and hours. Besides their primary problems, Marx insisted, the unions must learn to act as conscious organising centres of the working class in the interests of its complete emancipation. They must assist any social or political movement which aspires to this goal. They must regard themselves as fighters and representatives of the entire working class and must act accordingly; they should attract into their ranks all the workers. They must be indefatigably solicitous about the interests of the workers in the most poorly paid branches of industry, as, for instance, the farm labourers who, owing to the peculiarity of the conditions under which they work, are condemned to impotence. The trade unions must convince the entire world, that not only are they not narrow and selfish, but that, on the contrary, their objective is the setting free of oppressed millions.

Altogether, the debates at the Geneva Congress concerning trade unions were of great interest. The London delegates defended their position very ably. To them the resolution was a mere deduction from Marx's exhaustive report which, unfortunately, was known only to them. Even when the questions that were to be brought before the Congress had been discussed by the General Council, there sprang up serious disagreements. Marx, therefore, proceeded to deliver before the Council the detailed report in which he had clarified the significance of trade unions in the capitalist process of production. He took advantage of this opportunity to present to his audience, in a very popular form, his new theory of value and surplus value, to explain to them the interrelation of wages, profits, and prices. The minutes of these meetings of the General Council impress one with their profound seriousness of which many a learned bourgeois institution might be envious. The weight of all this scholarship and science was being offered in the service of the working class.

Not less skillfully did the London delegates defend Marx's resolution concerning the eight-hour day. In contradistinction to the French delegates, they maintained together with Marx that a condition precedent to any further efforts to improve and liberate the working class and without which all efforts would be futile was a legislative limitation of the length of the working day. It was essential to restore the health and the physical energy of the working class—the vast majority of each nation—and also to insure them the possibility of intellectual development, social communion, and political activity. The Congress, on the recommendation of the General Council, declared the eight-hour day as the legislative maximum. This limiting of the workday to eight hours was one of the demands of the workers in the United States. The Geneva Congress incorporated this demand into the platform of the working class of the whole world. Night work was allowed only in exceptional cases, in branches of industry and certain professions definitely specified by the law. The ideal was the elimination of all night work.

It is regrettable that Marx did not expatiate upon the question of woman labour in his report. He deemed it sufficient to say that the entire paragraph dealing with a shorter workday applied to all mature workers, women as well as men, with the additional provision that women were not to be admitted to any night work, or to any other work which would be ruinous for the female organism, or which would subject it to the action of poisonous or generally harmful substances. And since the majority of the French and Swiss delegates had declared themselves against any female labour, the Congress found it easy to accept Marx's thesis and to pass the resolution proposed by the Frenchmen. Thus the result was that it would be best to prohibit woman labour, but since it was still in use, it was necessary to keep it within the limits suggested by Marx.

Marx's propositions pertaining to child and adolescent labour were adopted in toto without any Proudhonist additions or modifications. Here it was suggested that the tendency of modern industry to attract children and adolescents of both sexes into a participation in the great tasks of social production was progressive, wholesome, and legitimate, despite the fact that under capitalism it degenerated into a horrible evil. In a rationally organised society, Marx thought, every child from the age of nine upward must engage in productive labour, just as no physically able adult can be released from a submission to the law of nature which demands physical and mental work from those who want to live. In connection with this question Marx proposed an elaborate programme to combine physical and mental labour. Spiritual and physical development plus a technical education which would give the children a grasp of the scientific principles involved in modern production—all this entered into his plan.

In his report Marx also touched upon the problem of co-operatives. He here took occasion not merely to destroy the illusions concerning pure co-operatives, but to point out the conditions antecedent to a successful co-operative movement.   As in the Inaugural Address, here too he preferred producers' to consumers' co-operatives.

"Restricted, however, to the dwarfish forms into which individual wage slaves can elaborate it by their private efforts, the co-operative system will never transform capitalistic society. To convert social production into one large and harmonious system of free and co-operative labour, *general social changes* are wanted, *changes of the general conditions of society,* never to be realised save by the transfer of the organised forces of society, viz: the state power from capitalists and landlords to the producers themselves."

We see that here too Marx was emphasising the necessity for the working class to win political power for itself.

The project of the Constitution, with which we have already become acquainted, was accepted without any modifications.   The efforts of the French delegates, who had already raised this question at the London conference, to interpret the word "work" to mean only physical work and thus to exclude the representatives of intellectual labour, met with a strong opposition.   The English delegates declared that should such a proposition be adopted, Marx, who had done so much for the International, would be among the first ones to be shut out.

The Geneva Congress effected a colossal propaganda weapon.   All the resolutions passed by this Congress which formulated the basic demands of the proletariat and which were almost exclusively written by Marx, entered into the practical minimum programmes of all working-class parties. The Congress met with warm response from all countries, including Russia.   It was immediately after the Geneva Congress, which had given such a powerful stimulus to the development of the international labour movement, that the International won great popularity for itself.   Some bourgeois-democratic organisations directed their attention to the International, intending to utilise it for their own purposes.

At the next Congress, in Lausanne (1867), a struggle broke out as to whether the new international society, the League for Peace and Freedom, should be permitted to participate in the next Congress. Those who were for participation won. Only at the following Congress, at Brussels (1868), did the point of view of the General Council triumph. It was decided to suggest to the League that it join the International, and that its members enter as a section of the International.

Marx was not present at these two Congresses either. Before the Lausanne Congress completed its work, the first volume of *Capital* was published. The Brussels Congress, at the suggestion of the German delegation, passed a resolution which urged the workers of the different countries to study *Capital*. The resolution pointed out that to Marx belonged the honour of being "the first economist who subjected capital to a scientific analysis and who reduced it to its basic elements."

The Brussels Congress also took up the question dealing with the influence of machinery on the conditions of the working class, strikes, and private ownership of land. Resolutions were adopted in a spirit of compromise. Nevertheless it was here that the point of view of socialism, or collectivism as it was then called, won over the French delegates. The necessity for a transition to collective ownership of the means of transportation and communication as well as of land was now clearly recognised. In its final form this resolution was adopted by the Congress at Basle (1869).

Since the Lausanne Congress the central political question in the International was war and its prevention. After the war of 1866, after Prussia's victory over Austria, the opinion was current that the inevitable consequence would be an armed conflict between France and Prussia. In 1867 the relations between these two countries reached a crucial stage. Napoleon's position became very insecure as a result of the unsuccessful colonial adventures into which he plunged in the hope of raising his prestige. At the instigation of several powerful financiers he contrived an expedition into Mexico. This provoked great irritation in the United States, which guarded most jealously against any infringement of the Monroe Doctrine. Napoleon's project came to a disgraceful end. Things had to be patched up in Europe. But there, too, failure haunted him. Having been compelled to make concessions in internal politics, he was hoping that a successful annexation in Europe which would round out the dominions of France would doubtless strengthen his position. Thus in 1867 there arose the Luxembourg Affair. After various unsuccessful attempts to lay hands on some territory on the left bank of the Rhine, Napoleon tried to buy from Holland the Grand Duchy of Luxembourg. Up to 1866 it had belonged to the German Union, but it was ruled by the King of Holland. A Prussian garrison which had formerly been stationed there was forced to leave. News of the bargain between Napoleon and Holland created great commotion among the German patriots. There were rumours of war. Napoleon, calculating that he was not yet fully ready for it, turned back. His prestige suffered a crucial blow. He again had to recede before the rising wave of opposition.

Toward the time of the Brussels Congress the situation in Europe became so acute that war seemed imminent. The feeling prevailed that it would break out as soon as France and Prussia completed their preparations and found a convenient pretext. The perplexing problem of how to prevent the war, which, it was well understood, would seriously injure the interests of the French and the German workers, was uppermost in the minds of the proletariat. The proletarian movement was growing rapidly, particularly on the continent. Therefore the International, which by 1868 had developed into a redoubtable force at the head of the international workers' movement, could not help becoming greatly involved in the question. After a series of heated debates in which some insisted that in case of war, it would be necessary to call a general strike, while others maintained that only socialism could bring an end to all war, the Brussels Congress adopted a rather absurd resolution which was the result of a compromise.

But since, toward the summer of 1869, the phantom of war had temporarily disappeared, economic and social problems rose to the top at the Basle Congress. The question concerning the co-operative ownership of all of the means of production which had already been superficially discussed by the Brussels Congress, was now for the first time put squarely before the delegates. Those who were opposed to private ownership of land won a sweeping victory. The followers of Proudhon were irrevocably swamped. New dissensions, however, arose at the Congress. It was at Basle that the famous Bakunin first made his appearance as the representative of a separate movement.

Where did he come from? We have already met him in Berlin at the beginning of the forties. We know that he had been influenced by the same philosophic currents which had influenced Marx and Engels. In 1848 he was connected with those of the German emigrants in Paris who had organised a revolutionary legion in order to invade Germany. During the revolution itself he was in Bohemia where he was trying to unite the Slav revolutionists. He later took a part in the insurrection of the Saxon revolutionists at Dresden, was arrested, condemned to death, but handed over to Nicholas I, who incarcerated him in the Schlüsselburg fortress. A few years later, in the reign of Alexander II, he was exiled to Siberia from which he escaped,

making his way through Japan and America back to Europe.
This happened in 1862. At first he plunged into Russian
affairs, joined Alexander Herzen (1812-1870),* wrote a few
pamphlets dealing with Slav and Russian questions and in
which he again insisted upon the necessity of a revolutionary
alliance of the Slavs, and made an unsuccessful attempt to
join the Polish insurrection. In 1864 he met Marx in London, from whom he learned of the founding of the International and to whom he promised his co-operation. He left
for Italy, however, where he became engrossed in something
entirely different. Bakunin now held the same view that he
had in 1848, that is that Marx exaggerated the importance
of the working class. According to him, the intelligentsia,
the student class, the representatives of the bourgeois democracy, particularly from among the middle classes, were
a much stronger revolutionary element. While the International was struggling with the difficulties it was at first
encountering and was gradually becoming the most influential
international organisation, Bakunin was trying to organise
his own revolutionary society in Italy. He then migrated to
Switzerland, and there joined the bourgeois League for Peace
and Freedom, and was even elected to the central committee
of that organisation. In 1868 he left the League, but instead of joining the International, he and his friends founded
a new society, the International Social-Democratic Alliance,
which came to be generally known as the Alliance.

The new society took a highly revolutionary stand. It
declared implacable war upon God and the State. It demanded of its members that they be atheists. The economic
programme was not distinguished by any particular clarity.
It demanded the economic and social levelling of all classes.
Despite its revolutionary character, the new organisation did
not even propose a consistent socialist programme; it confined itself to a demand for the abolition of the right of
inheritance. Anxious not to frighten away members of other

classes, it was careful not to stress its definite class character. The new society applied to the General Council that it be taken into the International as a separate organisation, with its own constitution and its own programme.

We are now approaching the most embarrassing point. Since Marx wielded a great influence in the General Council, he is usually held responsible for all the decisions that were made by the Council. Although this is not always correct, in this case Marx was chiefly responsible. Thus, if we should believe not only Bakunin's partisans but even those Marxists who are inclined to defend the great bungler, though very sincere revolutionist, Bakunin, Marx acted too precipitously when he insisted upon a decisive refusal. We, of course, are not so soft-hearted as to feel that the refusal to admit into the International a group that was guilty of hobnobbing with the bourgeoisie was too peremptory.

Let us recall another circumstance. Bakunin sent the programme of the new Alliance to Marx; he also mailed a personal letter under separate cover. This was about four years after Bakunin had written from Italy promising to work for the International. It was now disclosed that not only did he not keep his promise, but that he even exerted all his strength in favour of a bourgeois movement. True, he wrote that he now understood better than he ever had before how right Marx was in having chosen the broad highway of economic revolution; he ridiculed those who wandered astray along the path of purely national and political enterprises. He added with pathos:

"Since taking leave solemnly and publicly from the bourgeoisie at the Berne Congress, I no longer know any other society, any other environment, than the world of the workers. My country is now the International, of which you are one of the most important founders. So you see, my dear friend, that I am your disciple, and proud of my title."

This letter always evokes from Bakunin's friends tears of tenderness and a feeling of indignation against the heartless Marx who so relentlessly pushed away the hand that was stretched out to him.   Even Mehring remarked that there were no reasons to doubt the sincerity of these assurances.

We do not wish to doubt Bakunin's sincerity.   But let us try to place ourselves in Marx's predicament.   He was, to be sure, a hard man, but even Mehring would have to admit that up to the end of 1868 his attitude toward Bakunin was that of extreme tolerance.   The mere reading of it should make it plain why this sentimental letter should have appeared very unconvincing to Marx.   It was written not by a youngster, but by a man who was in his fifties, who once joined the "proletarian world" only to desert it in favour of the "bourgeois world."   Now, after having bothered with it for four years, and after having become completely disenchanted, he wished to stride "along the broad highway" again by joining the International, and advanced the most incongruous claims.   Marx, who had accepted Bakunin too trustingly in 1864, was now more careful.   He was proved to have been right.

When the General Council categorically refused Bakunin's request, the latter announced that his society resolved to disband and to transform its sections, which would continue to hold to their own theoretical programme, into sections of the International.   The General Council agreed to admit the sections of the former Alliance only on a common basis.

It would seem that everything turned out well.   But no; very soon Marx developed well-founded suspicions that Bakunin had simply deceived the General Council, that having officially disbanded his society, in reality he left its central organisation intact for the purpose of subsequently capturing the International.   This is the crux of the whole controversy.   We might admit that Marx was not a good-natured man, and that Bakunin was very good, even angelic

This is beside the point. We have known for a long time that Bakunin was guilty of sundry little sins. All men are sinful. Bakunin's defenders have to answer definitely: Was there or was there not such a secret organisation in existence? Did or did not Bakunin permit himself to deceive the General Council when he assured it that he had disbanded his organisation?

Notwithstanding our love for Marx, we would agree with Bakunin's friends in their assertion that Bakunin was maliciously slandered, had his friend, the historian of the International, the late Guillaume, proved that all this was mere fiction. Unfortunately, the Alliance continued to exist and to conduct a stubborn battle with the International. The lovable and good Bakunin did not hesitate to resort to any means which he deemed necessary for the accomplishment of his ends. We shall not hold it against him. Yet it appears ridiculous to see his admirers endeavour to make of him a man who never had recourse to questionable means and who, as one of his admirers assures us, was never guilty of any insincerity.

What then was the end which Bakunin felt would justify all the means? The destruction of bourgeois society, the social revolution—this was what Bakunin aspired to. But Marx's goal was precisely the same. The discrepancy must have arisen in a different domain. In reality this sharp divergence between Marx and Bakunin involves the methodology of revolution.

First destroy, and then everything will take care of itself. Destroy—the sooner, the better. It would be sufficient to stir up the revolutionary intelligentsia and the workers embittered through want. The only thing needed would be a group composed of determined people with the demon of revolution in their souls. This was essentially the whole of Bakunin's teachings. On the surface it resembled Weitling's teachings. But the resemblance was only superficial, as was its resemblance with Blanqui's teachings. The crux of the matter was that Bakunin did not want even to hear of the proletarian seizure of power. He denied any form of political struggle insofar as it had to be conducted on the ground of the existing bourgeois society and was concerned with the creation of more favourable conditions for the class organisation of the proletariat. That was why Marx and all the others who deemed the political struggle and the organisation of the proletariat for the conquest of political power indispensable, appeared to Bakunin and his disciples as wretched opportunists who hindered the coming of the social revolution. That was also why the Bakuninists were so ready to seize the opportunity of representing Marx as a man who in order to materialise his ideas would not hesitate to forge the Constitution of the International. Publicly, in circulars and letters, the Bakuninists abused Marx in the most vile language; they did not disdain anti-semitic acts, or even such absurd charges as, for instance, Marx's being the agent of Bismarck.

Bakunin had connections in Italy and Switzerland. In the French region of Switzerland particularly he had many followers. We cannot at this point go into a detailed study of the causes of this phenomenon. His propaganda was particularly successful among the imported labourers and the skilled watchmakers who were beginning to suffer from the competition of the developing industries.

Bakunin came to the Basle Congress backed by a considerable group. As often happens in such cases, the first skirmish broke out on entirely different grounds. Bakunin, who had always been vehemently opposed to any opportunism, was especially pertinacious in demanding the immediate abolition of the inheritance right. The delegates from the General Council insisted that such a measure was, as had been indicated in the *Communist Manifesto*, important merely as a transition measure which the proletariat would realise on seizing political power. Meanwhile it would be sufficient to attain a greater tax on wealth and a limited right of inheritance. Bakunin, however, took neither logic nor circumstances into consideration. For him this demand was important from the propaganda point of view. When it came to a vote neither of the resolutions had enough of a majority. Another conflict arose between Bakunin and Liebknecht. It happened that at the Basle Congress a new and significant German group made its appearance for the first time. About this time Wilhelm Liebknecht and August Bebel, after a furious factional struggle with Schweitzer, had succeeded in organising a separate party which had adopted at its constituent convention at Eisenach (1869) the programme of the International. Bakunin's activity in the League for Peace and Freedom and his old Pan-slavic views were thoroughly thrashed out and unfavourably criticised in the central organ of this party. Mehring points out that Marx personally expressed himself against this severe criticism, but, as we have seen in the Vogt episode, he was always held responsible for any act of the Marxists. Bakunin utilised the Congress to avenge himself on Liebknecht. The whole affair ended in a temporary reconciliation.

The next Congress was supposed to take place in Germany. It never convened. Immediately after the Basle Congress the political atmosphere became so dense, that an outbreak of war could be expected at any moment. Bismarck, one of the greatest tricksters in the history of the world, cleverly duped his former teacher, Napoleon. Having thoroughly prepared Germany for war, he so turned the tables that in view of the whole world, France appeared the aggressor.

When war actually did break out (July 19, 1870), it was quite unexpected. Neither the French nor the German workers found themselves able to prevent it. A few days after the declaration of war (July 23) the General Council published the proclamation written by Marx.

It began with a quotation from the Inaugural Address of the International in which was condemned

"a foreign policy in pursuit of criminal designs, playing upon national prejudices and squandering in piratical wars the people's blood and treasure."

Then followed a scathing indictment of Napoleon. Marx presented a compact picture of his fight against the International which became even more vehement after the French Internationalists had increased the scope of their violent agitation against Napoleon. Whichever side wins, added Marx, the last hour of the Second Empire had struck. The end of the Empire like its beginning will be a parody.

But was the guilt only Napoleon's? Not in the least. We must bear in mind that the various governments and the ruling classes of Europe had for eighteen years aided Bonaparte in playing the comedy of a reconstructed Empire.

Marx, a German himself, severely attacked his own country. From the German point of view this was a war of defence. But who had placed Germany in a situation which would require defence? Who evoked in Napoleon the temptation to attack Germany? Prussia. She had entered into an agreement with Napoleon against Austria. Should Prussia be defeated, France would flood Germany with French soldiers. But what had Prussia herself done after her victory over Austria? Instead of opposing enslaved France with a liberated Germany, she not only preserved all the charms of the old Prussian régime, but she even grafted onto it all the characteristic features of the Bonaparte régime.

The first decisive phase of the war terminated with amazing rapidity. The French army proved to be entirely unprepared. Contrary to the boastful declaration of the French Minister of War that everything was ready to the

last button, it became evident that if there really were buttons there was nothing to which these buttons could be attached. In about six weeks the regular French army was
defeated. On September 2, Napoleon had already given up
both himself and the great fortress of Sedan. On September
4, a republic was declared in Paris. Notwithstanding Prussia's declaration that she was fighting the Empire, the war
continued. It passed into the second, more prolonged and
more stubborn phase.

Immediately upon the proclamation of a Republic in
France, the General Council issued its second Manifesto concerning the war (September 9, 1870). It was again written
by Marx, and by its profound analysis of the historic moment, and its veritable prophetic insight, it represented one
of the most inspired pieces of Marx's writings.

We shall recall now that Marx had prognosticated even
in the first Manifesto that this war would lead to the destruction of the Second Empire. The second Manifesto
started out with a reference to this forecast. Not less correct was the criticism he had previously made of Prussian
foreign policy. The so-called defensive war degenerated into
a war on the French people. Long before the fall of Sedan
and the capture of Napoleon, as soon as the incredible dis-
integration of Bonaparte's army had become a known fact,
the Prussian military camarilla declared itself in favour of
a policy of conquest. Marx exposed the hypocritical behaviour of the liberal German bourgeoisie. Utilising the information supplied by Engels, who as a specialist had been
assiduously following up the development of the war and
had foretold the fall of Sedan, Marx exposed the fallacious
military arguments advanced by Bismarck and the Prussian
generals in justification of the annexation of Alsace and
Lorraine.

Being opposed to any annexations or indemnities, he maintained that such a forced peace would lead to another war.

France would want to regain what she had lost and would seek an alliance with Russia. Tsarist Russia which had lost its hegemony after the Crimean War would again become the arbiter of the destinies of Europe. This inspired prophecy, this foresight of the direction European history would take, is a striking and practical proof of the essential truth of the materialist conception of history. It is concluded in the following words:

"Do the Teuton patriots really believe that liberty and peace will be guaranteed to Germany by forcing France into the arms of Russia? If the fortune of her arms, the arrogance of success, and dynastic intrigue lead Germany to a dismemberment of France, there will then only remain two courses open to her. She must at all risks become the *avowed* tool of Russian aggrandisement, or, after some short respite, make again ready for another "defensive" war, not one of those new-fangled "localised" wars, but a *war of races*—a war with the combined Slavonian and Roman races."

Our contemporary German patriots were fated to see this prophecy come true to the last letter.

The Manifesto was concluded with an exposition of the practical problems that were then confronting the working class. The German workers were urged to demand an honourable peace and the recognition of the French Republic. The French workers, who were in even more difficult straits, were advised to watch the bourgeois republicans vigilantly and to utilise the Republic for the purpose of rapidly developing their class organisation and achieving their emancipation.

Immediate events fully justified Marx's distrust of the French republicans. Their contemptible conduct and their readiness to enter into an agreement with Bismarck rather than make the slightest concession to the working class, brought about the Paris Commune (March 18 to May 29, 1871). After a heroic struggle that lasted three months, this first experiment in the dictatorship of the proletariat under most unfavourable conditions, failed. The General Council was not in a position to give the Frenchmen the necessary help. The French and German armies cut Paris from the rest of France and the rest of the world. The Commune, indeed, awakened universal sympathy. There were revolutionary responses even in remote Russia.

During the existence of the Commune Marx tried to keep up communication with Internationalists in Paris. A few days after the defeat of the Commune Marx wrote at the request of the General Council the now famous Address.[3] He stepped forth in defence of the Paris communards who were maligned by the entire bourgeois press. He showed that the Paris Commune was a colossal step forward in the evolution of the proletarian movement, that it was the prototype of the proletarian state which would undertake the realisation of communism. Long before, as a result of the experience of the Revolution of 1848, Marx had come to the conclusion that the working class, after having seized power, could not simply lay hold of the bourgeois apparatus of the state, but that it would first have to demolish this bureaucratic machine and the police force upon which it rested. The experience of the Commune proved to him the soundness of his conviction. It proved that having seized power, the proletariat was forced to create its own machinery of state adapted to its own needs. The same experience of the Commune also showed that the proletarian state cannot exist within the limits of even a central city. The power of the proletariat must embrace the whole country for it to have any chances of becoming strengthened; it must sweep over a number of capitalist countries in order to be assured of a final victory.

Bakunin and his followers arrived at entirely different

[3] The Address first issued May 30, 1871, was later published under the title *The Civil War in France.*

conclusions. Their opposition to politics and the state became even more fervent. They urged the creation of communes in separate towns as soon as possible; these communes would inspire other towns to follow suit.

The defeat of the Commune brought about very unfavourable consequences upon the International itself. The French labour movement was paralysed for a few years. It was represented in the International by a host of communard refugees amongst whom bitter factional strife was raging. This strife was carried over into the General Council.

The German labour movement also suffered a serious setback. Bebel and Liebknecht, who protested against the annexation of Alsace-Lorraine, and who had declared their solidarity with the Paris Commune, were arrested and condemned to confinement in a fortress. Schweitzer who had lost the confidence of the party was forced to leave it. The followers of Liebknecht and Bebel, the so-called Eisenachers, continued to work independently of the Lassalleans.[4] These began to draw nearer to each other only after the government had swooped down with equal ferocity upon the two conflicting factions. The International thus lost support from the two greatest countries on the continent.

Moreover, there was a break in the English labour movement too. The war between the two most industrialised continental countries had benefited the English bourgeoisie not less than the last European war benefited the American. It was able now to give some share of its enormous profits to numerous workers in the chief industries. The trade unions gained a greater freedom of action. Several of the old laws that had aimed against the unions were abolished. All this had its effect on a few of the members of the General Council, which had been playing an important part in the trade-

[4] The two groups, the first, adherents of Marx, and the other, followers of Lassalle, continued their separate existence until they were united at the Gotha Congress in 1875.

union movement. To the extent with which the International was becoming more radical, to the same extent were many of the unions growing more and more moderate. Utilising their position for personal advantages, they continued to be members of the General Council only in form. The Commune and the bitter attacks it caused to be brought upon the International frightened them. Although the Manifesto dealing with the Paris Commune had been written by Marx at the request of the General Council, these members hastened to renounce their association with it. This caused a schism in the English section of the International.

These were the circumstances under which in September, 1871, a conference of the International was called in London. Two chief questions were taken up at this conference, one of which was the perplexing question concerning the struggle on the political field. In connection with this, the question of Marx's forging the Constitution of the International, which was pressed by the Bakuninists, was again taken up. The answer given by the resolution adopted, left not a shadow of a doubt. It indicated the complete defeat of the Bakuninists. As it is not widely known, we shall cite the concluding paragraphs:

"In presence of an unbridled reaction which violently crushes every effort at emancipation on the part of the working men, and pretends to maintain by brute force the distinction of classes and the political domination of the propertied classes resulting from it; . . .

"That this constitution of the working class into a political party is indispensable in order to insure the triumph of the social Revolution and its ultimate end—the abolition of classes;

"That the combination of forces which the working class has already effected by its economical struggles ought at the same time to serve as a lever for its struggles against the political powers of landlords and capitalists—

"The Conference recalls to the members of the International:

"That in the militant state of the working class, its economical movement and its political action are indissolubly united."

The conference had to encounter the Bakuninists on another score. The conviction that, despite Bakunin's protestations, his secret society continued to exist became firmly established in the General Council. The conference therefore adopted a resolution which prohibited any organisation with an independent programme to function within the body of the International. In connection with this the conference again took cognisance of the Bakuninists' declaration that the Alliance was disbanded and announced that the incident was closed.

But there was still another regulation which was intended to cause the discomfiture of Bakunin and his Russian followers. The conference resolved to declare in the most categorical manner that the International had nothing to do with the Nietchayev affair, that Nietchayev had falsely appropriated and utilised the name of the International.*

This decision was directed exclusively at Bakunin, who, as was well known, had been for a long time connected with Nietchayev, the Russian revolutionist who had fled from Russia in March, 1869. In the Fall of the same year Nietchayev returned to Russia and with Bakunin's authority organised a special Bakuninist group. Suspecting a certain student, Ivanov, of being a government spy, Nietchayev, aided by some of his comrades, murdered him and again fled to Europe. Those arrested in connection with this affair were put on trial in the summer of 1871. At the trial the prosecution made public many documents in which there was hopeless confusion as to the relation of Bakunin's society and its Russian branch with the International. It is enough to compare these documents with Bakunin's writings definitely to establish their authorship. These documents differed from his proclamations addressed to his European comrades by their greater frankness. The passages corrected and added by Nietchayev could be easily distinguished by the greater coarseness and carelessness of presentation.

This affair has been generally interpreted in the following way. Bakunin, it had been claimed, fell under the influence of Nietchayev who tricked him and used him for his own purposes.

Indeed, Nietchayev, a poorly educated man, who rejected all theory as sterile, was endowed with extraordinary energy, an iron will, and an unshakable devotion to the revolution. At the trial and in prison he showed his staunch manliness and his unquenchable hatred for the oppressors and the exploiters of the people. Ready to do anything, regarding any means good if he thought they would help him reach the goal to which he had dedicated his life, he never stooped to baseness for personal reasons. In this respect he was incomparably superior to Bakunin, the latter never having hesitated to enter into any deals if they furthered his personal aims. Nietchayev's moral superiority is beyond doubt. Everything points to the fact that Bakunin himself was fully conscious of this, else how could Bakunin respect and value so highly a man who was his intellectual inferior.

Yet it would have been naïve to deduce from all this that Nietchayev had imposed his revolutionary views on Bakunin. The converse is more nearly the truth; he was a disciple of Bakunin. But while our apostle of ruin proved himself to be an inconsistent character and an unstable revolutionist, Nietchayev was distinguished by his iron consistency; he made all the practical deductions from the theoretical propositions of his master. When Bakunin told him that he, Bakunin, could not refuse to do the work he had undertaken (a translation of *Capital*) because he had received money in advance, Nietchayev offered to free him of this obligation. This he accomplished in a very simple fashion. He wrote to the intermediary between Bakunin and the publisher demanding in the name of the revolutionary committee, "The People's Revenge," that the gentleman leave Bakunin alone if he did not wish to be killed.

Since, instead of the workers engaged in large industries, he had always stressed the *lumpenproletariat* as the real carriers of the social revolution, since he had regarded criminals and robbers as the most desirable elements to be attracted into the revolutionary ranks, his disciple, Nietchayev, quite consistently arrived at the conclusion that it was necessary to organise a group of desperadoes in Switzerland for the purposes of expropriation. Bakunin finally parted with his disciple, not because of a difference in principles, but because he was awed by Nietchayev's directness. Bakunin never dared to make this separation public; Nietchayev was in possession of too many compromising documents.

Immediately after the London Conference a still more savage battle broke out. The Bakuninists declared open war against the General Council. They accused it of shuffling the conference and of foisting upon the International the dogma of the necessity of organising the proletariat into a special party for the purpose of gaining political power. They demanded another Congress where this question would be definitely settled.

This Congress for which both parties had been preparing most feverishly, convened in September, 1872.* For the first time Marx was present in person. Bakunin was absent. The resolution of the Conference dealing with political action was ratified. There was one small addition which was lifted verbatim from the Inaugural Address of the International. It read:

"Since the owners of land and capital are always using their political privileges to protect and perpetuate their economic monopolies and to enslave labour, the great duty of the proletariat is to conquer the political power."

A special commission which examined all the documents pertaining to the Alliance came to the conclusion that this society had been existing as a secret organisation within the International, and proposed Bakunin's and Guillaume's expulsion. The proposal was accepted.

The resolution dealing with Bakunin's expulsion declared that besides the above-mentioned grounds Bakunin was expelled for a "personal reason." This referred to the Nietchayev incident. It seems that the Congress had ample reasons for excluding Bakunin on purely political grounds. It is ludicrous, however, to turn this sad episode in which Bakunin was the victim of his own lack of character into a cause for terrible accusations against Marx. It is still more ludicrous when the whole affair is construed in the following manner. Bakunin, it is asserted, had done what many other literary men are doing—he had failed to perform the work for which the publisher had paid him. Was this swindling? Of course not. But when Bakunin's defenders insist that Marx should not have blamed Bakunin, then it seems that either they do not understand or they forget, that the question was not at all as to whether Bakunin did or did not return to the publisher the money he had received in advance. The question was much more serious. Where Bakunin and his friends saw merely a fickle yet pardonable transgression which resulted only in a loss to the publisher, the members of the commission who had all the documents at their disposal felt that it was a criminal misuse of the name of a revolutionary organisation which had been in the minds of most people connected with the International; a misuse for personal reasons, for the purpose of freeing himself from meeting his pecuniary obligations. Had the document which was in the hands of the commission been made public at that time, it would have afforded the greatest satisfaction to the bourgeois world. It was written by Nietchayev; its contents, however, were not only not contrary to Bakunin's principles, they were in fact in full harmony with them. We must add that Bakunin parted with Nietchayev not because of this affair but because it appeared to him that Nietchayev was ready to regard even him as an instrument for the attainment of revolutionary aims.   Bakunin's letters to his friends illustrate adequately how unceremoniously Bakunin would hurl not only political but also personal accusations at his opponents, among whom Marx was included.   We know now that it was Bakunin who was the author of the notorious guide for revolutionists which was attributed to Nietchayev and which, when made public at the trial, evoked general indignation in the ranks of the revolutionists.   Bakunin's friends obstinately denied his authorship; they piled it all up against Nietchayev.

The Hague Congress was ended with Engels' proposal that the permanent residence of the General Council be transferred to New York.   We have already seen that at this time the International lost its moorings not only in France, where since 1872 the mere belonging to the International was held to be a crime, and not only in Germany, but also in England. It was presumed that the transfer of the International would be a temporary one.   It turned out, however, that the Hague Congress was the last one that had any significance in the history of the International.   In 1876 the General Council in New York published the notice that the First International ceased to exist.[*]

CHAPTER IX

ENGELS MOVES TO LONDON. HIS PARTICIPATION IN THE GENERAL COUNCIL. MARX'S ILLNESS. ENGELS TAKES HIS PLACE. *Anti-Dühring.* THE LAST YEARS OF MARX. ENGELS AS THE EDITOR OF MARX'S LITERARY HERITAGE. THE RÔLE OF ENGELS IN THE SECOND INTERNATIONAL. THE DEATH OF ENGELS.

WE have thus concluded the history of the First International, and we had no occasion to make mention of Engels. The formation of the International was accomplished without him, and up to 1870 he took only an insignificant and an indirect part in it. During these years he had written a few articles for some English labour journals. He had also been aiding Marx for whom the first years of the International were again years of bitter poverty. Were it not for the help he obtained from Engels and the small inheritance which was left to him by his old friend, Wilhelm Wolff, to whom he had dedicated his *Capital,* Marx would hardly have been able to overcome penury and he surely would have had no time to prepare his monumental work for publication. Here is a touching letter in which Marx informs Engels that he had at last finished correcting the last page:

"At last," he writes, "this volume is finished. I owe it only to you, that this has been possible. Without your self-sacrificing aid it would have been impossible for me to go through the colossal labour on these three volumes. I embrace you full of thanks."

Engels has been accused of having been a manufacturer. This we must admit, but we should also add that he had become that for a short time. After his father's death in 1860, Engels continued to work in the capacity of a simple employee. Only in 1864 did he become a member of the firm and one of the directors of the plant. During all this time he was trying to rid himself of this "dog's trade." He was deterred by the thought not only of himself but of Marx. In this regard his letters written to Marx in 1868 are very interesting. In them he informed Marx that he was conducting negotiations about leaving the firm, but that he wanted to accomplish it in a way that would insure his own and Marx's economic independence. He finally succeeded in coming to an agreement with his partner. In 1869 he left his factory on conditions which enabled him to provide for his friend, thus definitely ridding Marx of the penury that had been weighing upon him. Only in September, 1870, did Engels manage to move back to London.

For Marx, Engels' arrival meant more than personal happiness; it meant considerable relief from the colossal labour which he was performing for the General Council. There were always a countless number of representatives of various nations whom he had either to meet in person or to correspond with. Engels was noted for his linguistic abilities since his youth. He knew how to write, and, as his friends jested he knew how to stammer, in twelve languages. He was therefore ideally equipped for taking charge of the correspondence with the various countries. Besides, his long business experience proved useful in that he, unlike Marx, brought efficiency and order into his work.

Engels took over this work as soon as he became a member of the General Council in order to spare Marx whose health was undermined by excessive poverty and privation. He also took upon himself still other parts of the work. An energetic man, Engels had long been craving for the opportunity to do this work, and judging by the minutes of the General Council, he very soon became one of its most diligent members.

But this circumstance had another side to it. Engels

moved to London after the struggle with the Bakuninists
had begun and had already made itself felt in the General
Council. Moreover, as we have seen, at this time there was
serious discord even among the Englishmen themselves. In
brief, this was a time of sharp conflict on the ground of
principles and tactics.

It is a matter of common knowledge that struggles along
purely doctrinal and tactical lines are invariably complicated by a strong admixture of the personal element—
likes and dislikes, sympathies and prejudices, etc. If such
a conflict breaks out within the boundaries of one region,
one effective way to stop it is a temporary change of quarters. Although this method is efficacious within the limits of
a district, a state, or even an entire country, it was utterly
inapplicable within the International. Altogether this method of resolving contradiction has only a limited significance.
It is much better to settle such contradictions either by way
of agreement or by way of separation.

We have already spoken of the objective causes which
brought on the disturbance within the English section of the
International. What some historians of the International,
and especially historians dealing with the English labour
movement, do not or cannot understand is that the General
Council which from 1864 to 1872 was directing the international labour movement, was at the same time also the directing organ of the English labour movement. And if international affairs affected the English movement, then the
converse was also true, that is, every change in the English
labour movement was bound to be reflected in the international functions of the General Council. We have pointed
out in the last chapter how, as a result of the concessions
made to the English workers in the years 1867-1871—the
right to vote for the city workers and the legalisation of
trade unions—the trade-union members of the General Council began to tend toward moderation. Eccarius, too, began

to incline in that direction; he now was a prosperous man and, as it not infrequently happens with workers, became much more tolerant with the bourgeoisie. But besides Eccarius, there were a number of other members of the General Council who disagreed with Marx.

The appearance of Engels as a member of the General Council, who was often forced to take the place of Marx added one more personal element to aggravate the already strained conditions. During the twenty years of his life in Manchester, Engels had lost almost all contact with the labour movement.

During all that time Marx had stayed in London, had kept up his relations with the Chartists, had written for their publications, and had taken part in the German labour circles and in emigrant life. He had been meeting the comrades, had delivered lectures, had often had serious altercations with them, but on the whole the relations with "father" Marx, as we see by the reminiscences written even by those who had parted with him politically, were warm, comradely, and full of love. Particularly warm relations had been established between the workers and Marx during the period of the International. The members of the General Council who had been observing Marx in his dingy apartment, who had seen him in need—he had not lived any better than any English worker—who had known him in the Council, who had always found him ready to throw up his studies, his beloved scientific work, in order to devote his time and his energy to the working class, regarded him with the profoundest respect. Without compensation, rejecting all ostentatious advantages, declining all honorary titles, he had laboured without stint.

With Engels it was quite different. The English members of the General Council did not know him at all. The other members knew him just as little. Only among the German comrades were there some who remembered him, but even there he had to work hard to win a position for himself. For to most members he was a rich man, a Manchester manufacturer, who, it was said, had twenty-five years previous written a good book in German about the English workers. Having mingled for about twenty years in an almost exclusively bourgeois environment, among stockmarket wolves and industrial hawks, Engels, who was always noted for his decorous behaviour, acquired even more fastidious manners. Always spick and span, always even, of cold exterior, invariably polite, with military mannerisms, he would not utter a strong word. He was hopelessly dry and cold.*

This was the description of Engels given by people who had known him in the forties. We know that in the editorial offices of the *Neue Rheinische Zeitung*, whenever Marx would be on leave of absence, Engels would provoke serious objections by his haughty air of intellectual superiority. Less impulsive than Marx, he was much more unendurable in his personal relations, and in contradistinction to Wilhelm Wolff and Marx who were ideal comrades and guides, repelled many workers.

Only gradually did Engels adjust himself to his new setting, and lose his former habits. In the meantime, and these were difficult years to boot, Engels, having to substitute for Marx more and more often, aggravated the already strained relations in the General Council. This may serve as an explanation why not only Eccarius but even Hermann Jung, an old collaborator of Marx, who for a long time had been the General Secretary of the International, had very close personal bonds with Marx and who had very willingly and most delicately been helping Marx to carry his onerous obligations, now abandoned the organisation.

The whole affair was, alas, not without fairy tales and gossip customary in such cases. As we have already stated, many people, just because they did not know Engels, could not understand why Marx loved and lauded his friend so much. It is enough to read the disgusting and vile reminiscences of Henry Mayers Hyndman (1842-1923), the founder of the English social-democracy, to see how base were their explanations. According to them, it appeared that Marx valued Engels' friendship so highly because the latter was rich and was providing for him. The conduct of several Englishmen was particularly contemptible; among them was a certain Smith, who later became the interpreter at the congresses of the Second International.* During the recent war he was like Hyndman, a notorious social-patriot. Engels could never forgive either him or the others their vilifying campaign against Marx. Shortly before his death Engels threw down the stairs the same Mr. Smith who now came to visit him.

But then, in the beginning of the seventies, this calumny in its most malignant forms, was spreading also among the German workers of the Lassallean persuasion, who were coming to London. But Engels' participation sharpened the schism not only in London. We know that outside of Russia Bakunin and his adherents concentrated their work in the Latin countries—Italy, Spain, Southern France, Portugal, the French and Italian parts of Switzerland. Italy was especially valued by Bakunin, for there was a predominance of the *lumpenproletariat*, the hobo-proletariat, in whom he discerned the cardinal revolutionary force. There was also the youth, which had no hope of making a career in bourgeois society. There, too, flourished banditry and robbery as forms in which the protest of the poor peasantry expressed itself. In other words, there the elements to which he was attaching such great importance in Russia—the peasantry, the hobo-proletariat, the robbers— were all greatly developed.

The main correspondence with these countries was carried on by Engels. This correspondence, as may be judged by a few preserved copies (the efficient Engels would always retain a copy for himself) was conducted in a spirit of relentless opposition to the Bakuninists.

The famous pamphlet on Bakunin's Alliance, which was a report of the commission of the Hague Congress, and which most caustically lashed and exposed the Bakuninist policy and tactics, was written by Engels and Lafargue. Marx contributed only to the concluding chapter, though he was, of course, in complete accord with the indictment of Bakuninism.

After 1873, Marx left the public arena. In this year he completed the second edition of the first volume of *Capital*, and was editing a French translation which was finally published in 1875. If we should add to this a postscript which he wrote for the old book about the Communist League, and the small article written for the Italian comrades it would make up the sum total of everything Marx had published up to 1880.* As much as his shattered health permitted him he continued to labour over his *magnum opus*, the first draft of which Marx had completed in the early sixties. But he did not succeed in making ready for publication even the second volume over which he was then labouring. We know now that the last manuscript which was incorporated in this volume was written in 1878. Any strenuous intellectual work was a menace to his overwrought brain. During these years Marx's family and Engels were in perpetual fear for Marx's life which was always threatened by a sudden stroke. The mighty organism, once capable of superhuman labour, was gradually becoming weaker. Engels' touching care, his efforts to do everything possible to restore his old friend to health, were of little avail. Before Marx lay his great work in the rough, and as soon as he would feel a trifle better, as soon as the danger of death would become more remote, as soon as the physicians would allow him to work a few hours a day, he would resume his labours. The consciousness that he would never be able to complete this work was a continuous torture to him. "To be incapable of work," Marx would say, "is to any human being who does not wish to be simply an animal the equivalent of a death sentence." After 1878 he was forced to give up all work on *Capital* in the hope that he would be able to return to it at some more auspicious time. This hope was not fulfilled. He was still able to make notes, he still kept up with the development of the international labour movement and took an active intellectual part in it, answering numerous inquiries which were coming to him from various countries. His list of addresses reached particularly imposing dimensions toward the beginning of the eighties. Together with Engels, who at this time took over most of the work, he again became a well-informed man, an expert on the rapidly developing labour movement within which the ideas of the *Communist Manifesto* were gaining ascendency. A great deal of credit in this matter was due to Engels who, in the seventies, and while Marx was still alive, was developing a very energetic activity.

The struggle between the Marxists and the Bakuninists in the First International has often been greatly exaggerated. There were indeed quite a few Bakuninists, but even among them there was a variety of elements, united only in their onslaught on the General Council. Things were much worse with the Marxists. Behind Marx and Engels there was only a small group of people, who were acquainted with the *Communist Manifesto* and who understood fully all the teachings of Marx. The publication of *Capital* was at the beginning of very little help. For the vast majority it was in the full sense of the words a granite rock at which they most diligently nibbled; that was all. The writings of the German socialists during the first half of the seventies, even the brochures written by Wilhelm Lieb-knecht, who was a student of Marx, show the deplorable state in which the study of Marxian theory was at that time. The pages of the central organ of the German party were often filled with the most grotesque mixture of various socialist systems. The method of Marx and Engels, the materialist conception of history, and the teaching about the class struggle—all this remained a sealed book. Liebknecht himself so little grasped the Marxian philosophy that he confused the dialectic materialism of Marx and Engels, with the natural-historical materialism of Jacob Moleschott (1822-1893), and Ludwig Büchner (1824-1899).

Finally, Engels took upon himself the task of defending and disseminating the tenets of Marxism, while Marx, as we have seen, was vainly trying to complete his *Capital*. Engels pounced now upon an article that especially appealed to him, now upon a fact of contemporary history in order that he might illustrate with individual cases the profound difference between scientific socialism and other socialist systems, or throw light on some obscure practical question from the point of view of scientific socialism, or show the practical application of his method.

Since the famous German Proudhonist Mülberger was publishing in the central organ of the German Social-Democracy a series of articles dealing with the housing question, Engels, seizing upon this as a good pretext showed the chasm that separated Marxism from Proudhonism (*Die Wohnungsfrage*). Besides this magnificent supplement to Marx's book, *Poverty of Philosophy*, he cast the lucid light of Marxism upon one of the chief factors determining the condition of the working class.

He republished his old work, the *Peasant War in Germany*,[1] with a new preface in order to illustrate to his young comrades the manner in which the materialist conception of history might be applied to one of the most impor-

[1] Recently published in English.

tant episodes in the history of Germany and the German peasantry.

When the German Reichstag was discussing the question of how the Prussian landowners made secure their profitable business of rendering the Germans into a habitually drunken people, Engels proceeded to write a brochure *Prussian Schnaps in the German Reichstag,* in which, besides exposing the desires of the Prussian junkers, he explained the historic rôle of Landlordism and Prussian junkerdom. All these works of Engels added to his other articles dealing with German history made it subsequently possible for Kautsky and Mehring to popularise, and develop in their works on German history, the basic ideas of Engels.

But Engels' greatest services belong to the years 1876 and 1877. In 1875 the Lassalleans and the Eisenachers had united on the basis of the so-called Gotha Programme—a poor compromise between Marxism and its distorted double, known by the name of Lassalleanism. Marx and Engels protested most vigorously, not because they were opposed to unification but because they demanded a change in the programme in accordance with their suggestions. They insisted, with very good reason that though unification was indubitably necessary, it nevertheless, was not at all desirable to adopt a bad programme as the theoretical foundation of this unification; that it would be preferable to postpone the adoption of a programme for a little while and to be satisfied in the meanwhile with a general platform fit for everyday practical work. In this affair August Bebel (1840-1913) and Wilhelm Bracke (1842-1880), were also opposed to Liebknecht.

Only a few months later Marx and Engels had occasion to be convinced that in the matter of theoretical preparation the two factions were on the same low level. Among the young members of the party, the intellectuals as well as the workers, the teachings of Eugen Dühring (1833-1901), the famous German philosopher and economist, were winning wide popularity.   At one time he had been assistant pro- fessor at the Berlin University, and had won great sym- pathy owing to his personality and the daring of his re- marks, unusual for a German professor.   Though blind, he lectured on the history of mechanics, on political economy and on philosophy.   His versatility was amazing; no doubt, he was a remarkable personality.   When he came out with his caustic criticism of the recognised socialist teachings and particularly those of Marx, his lectures made a tremendous impression.   To the students and the workers it appeared that his was a "voice of life in the realm of thought." Dühring emphasised the significance of action, of struggle, of protest; he stressed the political factor as against the economic one; he pointed out the importance of force and violence in history.   In his polemic he knew no restraints and abused profusely not only Marx but also Lassalle.   He was not even ashamed to cite the fact that Marx was a Jew, as an argument against him.

Engels hesitated for a long time before he decided to strike against Dühring.   He finally gave way to the solicitations of his German friends and in 1877 published in the *Vorwärts*, the central organ of the party, a series of articles in which he subjected Dühring's views to scathing criticism.   This provoked indignation even among some of his comrades in the party.   Dühring's followers, Eduard Bernstein (1850—),* the future theoretician of revisionism, and Johann Most (1846-1906), the future German-American anarchist, were the most outstanding.   At the convention of the German Social-Democrats a number of delegates, among whom was also the old Lassallean Walteich, attacked Engels merci- lessly.   It reached the point where a resolution was almost adopted which would prohibit the further publication of Engels' articles in the central organ of the party, which re- garded Marx and Lassalle as their teachers.

An inconceivable scandal would have resulted, had it not
been for one conciliator who proposed a clever way out
by suggesting that the publication of Engels' articles be
continued not in the central organ proper but in a special
supplement. This was passed.

These articles were collected and published in book form
in 1878 under the title *Herrn Eugen Dühring's Umwälzung
der Wissenschaft* [2] or, as it has later become known, *Anti-
Dühring.** It was epoch-making in the history of Marxism.
It was from this book that the younger generation which began its activity during the second half of the seventies
learned what was scientific socialism, what were its philosophic premises, what was its method. *Anti-Dühring* proved
the best introduction to the study of *Capital.* A perusal of
the articles written in those days by would-be Marxists reveals a view most awry of the problems and the methods of
Capital. For the dissemination of Marxism as a special
method and a special system, no book except *Capital* itself,
has done as much as *Anti-Dühring.* All the young Marxists
who entered the public arena in the early eighties—Bernstein, Karl Kautsky (1854—),† George Plekhanov (1857-
1918)—were brought up on this book.

But this book left its imprint not only on the upper layers
of the party. At the solicitation of the French Marxists,
Engels, in 1880, extracted a few chapters which were translated into the French and which became one of the most
famous Marxist books as widely read as the *Communist
Manifesto.* This was the well-known *Socialism—Utopian
and Scientific.* It was immediately translated into Polish,
and a year and a half later, into Russian. All this Engels
accomplished while Marx was still alive. Engels benefited by
his advice and even his co-operation. In *Anti-Dühring*, for
instance, Marx wrote one complete chapter.

---

[2] Published in part in an English translation under the title *Land-
marks of Scientific Socialism.*

At the beginning of the eighties a change took place in the European labour movement. Owing to Engels' tireless labours and his splendid popularising gifts, Marxism was steadily gaining ground. In 1876, in Germany, the Social-Democratic Party was declared illegal. After a temporary confusion Marxism began to rise to the top. Bebel shows in his reminiscences that it was the old men from London who played an important part in this turn of affairs, for they demanded, under the threat of a public protest, the discontinuance of what they called "the scandal" and the irreconcilable struggle against all attempts to enter into any relations with the bourgeoisie.

In France at the Marseilles Congress of 1879 a new labour party with a socialist programme was organised. Here a young group of Marxists, headed by the ex-Bakuninist, Jules Guesde (1845-1921), came to the fore. In 1880, it was decided to formulate a new programme. Guesde and his comrades went to London to see Marx, who was taking an active part in the working out of the programme. Refusing to subscribe to several of the points dealing with the practical aspect of the work on which the Frenchmen were insisting because of their local propaganda value, Marx proceeded to formulate the fundamental principles of the programme. He once more demonstrated his ability to comprehend the peculiarly French conditions by formulating a programme which would be understood by every Frenchman but from which the basic ideas of communism would follow with incontrovertible logic. The French programme served as the pattern for all the subsequent programmes—the Russian, the Austrian, the German Erfurt. After Guesde and Lafargue had composed their commentaries to this programme, Bernstein translated it into German and Plekhanov into Russian under the title, *What the Social-Democrats Want*. This book as well as Engels' brochure served as a text which was studied by the first Russian

Marxists and which was used in the teaching of Marxism in workingmen's circles.

Marx had also composed for the French comrades a detailed questionnaire as an aid in the investigation of the conditions of the working class. This appeared without Marx's signature. While the questionnaire drawn up by Marx for the Geneva Congress of 1866 contained only about fifteen queries, the new questionnaire was made up of over one hundred questions which covered to the minutest detail, the living conditions of the workers. It was one of the most exhaustive inquiries at the time and it could have been composed only by such a profound student of the labour movement as Marx. It offered additional proof of Marx's ability to approach concrete conditions, to comprehend concrete reality despite his reputed penchant for abstractions. The capacity for analysing reality and for arriving at general conclusions on the basis of such analysis does not yet signify the absence of reality, the soaring in nebulous abstractions.

Marx and Engels followed the development of the Russian Revolution very carefully. They studied the Russian language. Marx took it up quite late in life, but he mastered it sufficiently well to be able to read Dobrolyubov, Chernishevsky, and even such writers as Saltikov-Shchedrin, who were particularly difficult for a foreigner to understand.[3] Marx was already able to read the Russian translation of his *Capital*. His popularity in Russia was steadily on the increase, even after the Hague Congress. As the critic of bourgeois political economy he was regarded as a great authority and his influence, direct and indirect, was felt in most of the economic and political writings in Russia. Peter Lavrov (1823-1900), and his followers were under the direct influence of Marx, though they did manage to inject some idealist notions into Marxian materialism.

[3] Literary critics and sociological writers.

Later in their history, the Russian Bakuninists too regarded Marx with great respect. Some of the greatest Marxians, George Plekhanov, Vera Sassulitch (1851—), Paul Axelrod (1850–1928), Leo Deutsch (1855—),* were Bakuninists in their early years. Marx and Engels valued greatly the movement known by the name of *Narodnaya Volya* (the People's Will).[4]

There are a number of Marx's manuscripts and letters which show how carefully Marx studied Russian literature and Russian socio-economic relations. Having thoroughly mastered the data dealing with the state of agriculture in Russia, he did not merely point out the chief causes of Russian crop-failures, but he established the law of their periodicity. His deductions have been justified by history up to and including the last crop-failure in Soviet Russia. Much of the Russian material which Marx intended to utilise in his third volume in connection with the study of the agricultural question was destined to go to waste because of his failing health. The manuscript material left by Marx contains four drafts of a reply to an inquiry of Vera Sassulitch regarding the Russian system of communal landholding (*Mir*).[5]

The last year and a half of Marx's life was a slow process of dying. Before him he had the rough copy of a gigantic work to which he would turn as soon as he had a moment's respite. In the days of his prime, he had created the essential contours of a model, a draft, in which the basic laws of capitalist production and exchange were expressed. But he had not the strength left to transmit this into an organism as living as the first volume of *Capital*.

Finally, when fate brought down almost simultaneously

[4] This populist-socialist organisation was active in Russia during the seventies. The assassination of Alexander II on March 14, 1881, was the culmination of its activities.

[5] Discovered by Riazanov and recently published in *Marx-Engels Archiv.*, Vol. I, pp. 318-343.

the two heavy blows of the death of his wife and his daughter, upon his exhausted, disease-ridden, emaciated organism, it could not withstand the shock. The ferocious Marx was, strange as it may seem, a most devoted family man and most delicate in his personal contacts. On reading the letters Marx had written to his daughter, whose death affected him so much that his nearest friends feared a fatal relapse, one wonders where this stern man found such a spring of tenderness and sensitiveness.

Philistines and revolutionary novices are amazed and nonplussed when they read the last pages of Marx's life. It is not good, to be sure, when a revolutionist devotes even a part of his energy to things outside the revolution. A real revolutionist, according to those who are often only knights for an hour, ought all the time, every minute of his life, be on guard. He must be moulded of revolutionary adamant, aloof from all human emotions.

One should judge humanly. We all enjoy the thought that those whom we have regarded with great reverence and awe are after all people like ourselves, only a bit wiser, more educated, and more useful to the cause of the revolution. It was only in the old, pseudo-classical dramas that men were depicted as heroes: they walked and the mountains would tremble, they stamped their feet and the earth would crack; they even ate and drank like heroes.

Marx, too, has been frequently portrayed in the above manner. It is thus that he appears in the descriptions of him given by the lovely old Clara Zetkin, who is generally inclined to elevated and solemn tones. When Marx is thus represented, it seems that people forget that he himself, in answer to the question as to what was his favourite motto, replied, "I am a man, and nothing human is alien to me." Nor were sins alien to him, and he more than once regretted his excessive trust in some cases and his flagrant injustice in other. Some of his admirers found it easy to forgive

Marx his inveterate love for wine (Marx was a native of the Moselle district) but they found it more difficult to bear his incessant smoking. He himself would jestingly remark that the royalties he received from the sale of *Capital* were not enough to pay for the tobacco he had consumed while writing it. Owing to his poverty he would smoke the cheapest brands of tobacco; a great deal of life and health was thus puffed away by him. This was the cause of chronic bronchitis which became particularly malignant during the last years of his life.

Marx died on March 14, 1883. And Engels was right when on the day of Marx's death he wrote to the latter's old comrade, F. A. Sorge: [6]

"All phenomena, even the most terrible, which take place in accordance with natural laws, are not without their own consolation. Such is the case now. The art of healing could probably have added to his life a couple of years of vegetating existence, the life of a helpless man, maintained by physicians as a tribute to their own skill, and dying by inches instead of suddenly; but such a life Marx would hardly have endured. To live, confronted with his many unfinished tasks, and to suffer the pains of Tantalus at the thought of the impossibility of carrying them to a conclusion, would have been for him a thousand times more dreadful than the peaceful death that fell to his lot.

" 'Death is terrible not to the dying, but to the one who remains among the living,' it was his wont to reiterate, with Epicurus, but to see this mighty genius a ruin dragging on its existence for the greater glory of medicine and to hear the jibes of the philistines, whom, in the days of his flower, he had so mercilessly flayed—no, what has happened is a thousand times preferable; no, it will be a thousand times better, when, the day after to-morrow, we carry him out to the grave where his wife sleeps.

"In my opinion, after all he had lived through, which was

[6] F. A. Sorge was secretary of the First International after the transfer of its headquarters to New York in 1872. He was active in the German-American labour movement until his death in 1906.

clearer to me than to all the physicians, there was no alternative.

"Be this as it may. Humanity has grown shorter by a head, the most gifted head it has had at its disposal.

"The proletarian movement will go on, but the centre is gone, the centre whither in crucial moments Frenchmen, Russians, Americans, and Germans hastened for aid, where they always received the clear and irrefutable counsel, which could only be given by a genius in perfect command of his subject."

Engels was now confronted with some very harassing problems. A brilliant writer and one of the best stylists in the German language, a widely educated man yet at the same time a specialist in several domains of human knowledge, he, willy-nilly, receded to a secondary position while Marx was alive.

"I hope I may be permitted here to make a remark by way of personal explanation. Reference has frequently been made in recent days to my share in the formation of this theory, and I can therefore hardly avoid the necessity of here making, in a few words, a final statement on this subject.

"I cannot deny that I had an independent share before as well as during my forty years of work with Marx, in laying down as well as—more particularly—in the elaboration of the theory. But the overwhelming part of the basic and leading ideas especially in the domains of history and economics, as well as the final and keen statement of them belongs to Marx. What I contributed, Marx could have easily filled in without my aid, with the exception perhaps of two or three special branches of knowledge. But what Marx did, I could have never done. Marx stood higher, saw farther, had a wider, more comprehensive and swifter view than all of us. Marx was a genius; we were at most talents. Without him our theory would have been far from what it is now. It is therefore justly called by his name." [7]

Engels, in his own words, had now to play first fiddle; he had been playing second fiddle all his life and had always found great joy in the fact that the first fiddle was played

[7] F. Engels: *Ludwig Feuerbach und der Ausgang der Klassischen Deutschen Philosophie*, 1888, p. 43.

with such marvellous virtuosity by Marx. Both of them played from notes which only they could so easily read. The first Herculean task that fell to Engels was the collating of Marx's literary legacy. Contrary to the petty insinuations of an Italian professor, who had once presented himself to Marx and had showered upon him most flattering expressions of adulation, but who now dared to suggest in print that the references Marx had made in the first volume of *Capital* to the second and third volumes were merely calculated to deceive the public, Marx's papers revealed manuscripts for a second, third, and even fourth volume. Unfortunately, all this was left in such disorder that Engels, who was not in a position to devote his entire time to this task, was forced to work over these papers for a period of eleven years. Marx wrote very illegibly, using at times stenographic characters of his own invention. Shortly before his death, when it had finally become clear to him that he would not be able to finish his work, Marx remarked to his younger daughter that perhaps Engels would be able to do something with his papers.

Fortunately, Engels succeeded in completing the cardinal part of this work. He edited the second and third volumes. We might admit that besides Engels there was hardly a man would be capable of performing this great task. These volumes have some faults, but, as they are published now, the name of Engels fully deserves to stand beside that of Marx. There is very little hope that we may secure Marx's original manuscripts as they reached Engels. With the exception of the first volume, Marx's *Capital* is accessible to us only through Engels' version of it.

Formerly, particularly after the demise of the First International, Marx and Engels together had been performing the part of the erstwhile General Council. Now all the work of mediation and keeping up relations among various socialist groups, as well as the work of consultant and of purveyor of information, pressed as an ever-growing burden on Engels alone. Not long after the death of Marx, the international labour movement manifested vigorous signs of life. In 1886 there began talk about the organisation of a new International. But even after 1889, that is, after the first congress which organised the Second International but which did not provide for a permanent central bureau up to 1900, Engels was taking a very active part as litera-teur and adviser to the labour movements of well-nigh all the countries of Europe. The old General Council, which consisted of numerous members and of a number of secre-taries from the several countries, was now embodied in Engels. As soon as a new group of Marxists would spring up in any country, it would forthwith turn to Engels for counsel; and with his uncanny knowledge of languages he would manage, now correctly, now interspersed with some errors, to reply in the group's native tongue. He followed the labour movements in the different countries by reading their respective publications in the original. This took up a good deal of his time, but it enabled him to strengthen the influence of Marxism in those countries by his skillful application of Marx's formulæ to the specific conditions of each country. There is literally no country which was not served by Engels in his capacity of writer. We find him writing articles not merely for German and Austrian organs, not only for the French, but we see him writing a new introduction to the Polish translation of the *Communist Manifesto*, and helping the Spanish and Danish, the Bul-garian and Serbian Marxists with his counsel and sugges-tions.

The aid which Engels gave young Russian Marxists de-serves special mention. Since he knew the language he could keep in direct and immediate touch with Russian Marxian literature. And it was only because of his influence that, notwithstanding the enormous prestige of the *Narodnaya*

Volya, the Emancipation of Labour [8] group could so speedily establish ties with German Marxism. It was solely because of Engels that they could overcome the distrust which western Europe, and Germany especially, felt toward the labour movement and the Marxism of an Asiatic country like Russia. In 1889 Plekhanov made a special trip to London to see Engels and to acquaint him with the new tendencies in the Russian revolutionary movement. Engels even wrote a special article dealing with the foreign policy of Russian Czarism for the first Russian Marxist periodical.

Engels very soon beheld the fruits of his energetic activity. When the Second International was founded Engels did not take a direct part in the work of its congresses. He avoided public appearances and he confined himself to giving advice to those of his disciples who were now at the helm of the labour movement in various countries; they informed him of everything important that occurred, soliciting his advice and the sanction of his authority. Some parties won for themselves great influence which they maintained in the International, thanks to Engels' backing. Toward the end of his life this perpetual intercourse with only the heads of the leading parties of the different countries resulted in some inconsistencies. Thus, while he immediately rose against the infatuation of the French Marxists with the peasant question and defended the proletarian character of the programme, he capitulated before his German comrades, who fearing the revival of the law against socialists, persuaded him to modify the vigour of his introduction to Marx's study *The Class Struggles in France*—a brilliant application of the ideas of a relentless class struggle and the dictatorship of the proletariat.

In the introduction to the fourth German edition of the

---

[8] The first definitely Marxian group organised by Plekhanov, Sassulitch, Axelrod, Deutsch and others in 1883 which was the precursor of the Russian Social-Democratic Labor Party formed in 1898.

Communist Manifesto which he wrote on the first international celebration of the First of May (1890), Engels after pointing out the inspiring growth of the international labour movement, expressed his regrets that Marx was not alongside of him to see this with his own eyes. While Marx was known only to the advanced elements of the working-class movement, Engels, who knew the significance of advertising and revolted against the shroud of darkness which the capitalist press was trying to throw over Marx's *Capital*, but who shrank from any kind of self-advertising not less than his friend, did toward the end of his life become one of the most popular men in the international labour movement. He had occasion to convince himself of this when, surrendering to the insistence of his friends, he visited the European continent in 1893. Mass ovations and receptions, which Lassalle had once recommended not merely as a means of propaganda but also as a means of distinguishing, advertising and elevating the leaders above the mass—these assumed grandiose proportions simply because of the now colossal dimensions of the labour movement. A similar ovation was arranged for Engels at the Zurich Congress where he wished to be only a guest, and where only toward the end of the celebration, he was persuaded to deliver a short speech.

Engels, unlike Marx, retained his ability to work almost to the age of seventy-five. As late as 1895 he wrote an interesting letter to Victor Adler which contained suggestions as to how the second and third volumes of *Capital* should be read. At about the same time he also wrote an interesting supplement to the third volume. He was making ready to write the history of the First International. In the very heat of all this mental work he was overcome by a cruel sickness which finally brought his life to an end on August 5, 1895.

Marx was buried in London in one grave with his wife

and his grandchild. It is marked by a simple stone. When Bebel wrote to Engels that he intended to propose that a monument be erected on Marx's grave, Engels replied that Marx's daughters were unalterably opposed to this. When Engels died cremation was just beginning to come into vogue. Engels in his will asked that his body be cremated, and that his ashes be dropped into the sea. Upon his death the question arose as to whether his will should or should not be carried out. Many of his German comrades were reluctant to give up the idea of a grave and a worthy monument. Fortunately, there were enough comrades who insisted that his will be complied with. His body was burned, and the urn with the ashes was let down into the sea.

Both friends have left behind them a monument stronger than any granite, more eloquent than any epitaph. They have left us a method of scientific research, rules of revolutionary strategy and tactics. They have left an inexhaustible treasure of knowledge which is still serving as a fathomless source for the study and the comprehension of surrounding reality.

NOTES

Page 14

The term "Industrial Revolution" was used in France at least as early as the 1820s, in analogy to what was known as "The Revolution," the one of 1789. Friedrich Engels, using the term in 1844 and 1845, may well have met it in the French literature and have used it for the first time in the German language. Strangely enough, the term has not been noticed in English before 1884, when the economist Arnold Toynbee used it. Toynbee knew Marx's *Capital,* which uses the term in German (its English translation dates from 1886). See A. Bezanson, *Quarterly Journal of Economics,* 36 (1922), pp. 343-349; G. N. Clark, *The Idea of the Industrial Revolution* (Glasgow, 1953).

Page 20*

The statement that Napoleon "never, to the last days of his life, disdained the weapon of revolutionary propaganda" can be challenged. In the words of the Russian historian, E. Tarlé: "The invincibility of Napoleon's army disappeared when he abandoned the historically progressive mission that he had been fulfilling" (*Napoleon in Russia* [New York, 1942], p. 60).

Page 20†

Aleksandr Nikolaevich Radishchev (1749–1802) was a Russian nobleman, who, while abroad, became acquainted with French philosophy. In 1790 he published *Voyage from St. Petersburg to Moscow,* in which he called for the abolition of serfdom and the downfall of tsarism. He was sent to Siberia. After his return, again frustrated, he committed suicide.

Page 24

In lines 1 through 7 the author is speaking of the Reform Bill of 1832.

Page 26

Karl Schapper was first imprisoned in and then expelled from France.

Page 27

Marx was born May 2, 1818; Friedrich Engels, November 28, 1820.

Page 28

The former Holy Roman Empire, which disappeared in 1806, was a conglomerate of many German-speaking states. At the peace of Vienna many smaller states were eliminated; what remained as leading states were Prussia in the north and Austria in the south, as well as a host of other states, such as Saxony and Bavaria.

Page 32*

Wilhelm Liebknecht (1826–1900) was one of the founders of the German Social Democratic Party (1869).

Page 32†
The Paris League of the Just was disorganized after the Blanqui uprising of 1839, but recovered. There were branches of the League in Paris
through the 1840s; these, together with branches in other cities, became
part of the Communist League in 1847 (see note to p. 65).

Page 32‡
The Workers' Educational Society (*Arbeiterbildungsverein*), was not
"transformed" into a Communist organization, but the Communists, organized in the League of the Just, worked inside it. It was often called
the Communist Educational Society. It existed until 1916.

Page 34
This is not quite fair to Mehring. Mehring, in his biography of Marx, also
mentions the desire of Marx to avoid "the new persecutions."

Page 36
Here a crucial period in Marx's life has been omitted. He stayed in Bonn
only one year and then transferred to the University of Berlin, where
he "plunged passionately into his studies," as Riazanov writes. In Berlin
he joined the Young Hegelians. He stayed there until 1841, when he
moved back to Bonn to join his (then) mentor, Bruno Bauer.

Page 37*
Marx never studied at Jena; he obtained his doctoral degree *in absentia*
after sending in his dissertation on Greek materialism.

Page 37†
Engels did not meet Marx in the Berlin set of Young Hegelians. Marx
left Berlin in April 1841, and Engels arrived there in September 1841 for
his military service.

Page 37‡
Marx's grandfather was Marx Levi (d. 1798), rabbi at Treves, who
called himself Marx.

Page 39
Schelling was already in Berlin when Engels wrote his critique; it was
inspired by Engels' attendance at Schelling's inaugural oration in November 1841.

Page 49
This reference to Hindoo theology is obscure. The years 1897–1898 were
in the period when X-rays and radioactivity were discovered. Perhaps
Riazanov refers to spiritualism, then popular with such physicists as
W. Crookes and Oliver Lodge.

Page 61
While in Paris during 1844, Marx continued his critique of Hegel in a
study of his logic and in a re-evaluation of his concept of alienation. This
work remained in manuscript until Riazanov published it in Russian in
1927. It was later published in MEGA in the original German, and is
now known as the *Economic and Philosophic Manuscripts of 1844*. *The
Holy Family* was written after this, when Engels joined Marx in August
1844.

Page 63

This summary is a bit of a parody of Engels' account written from memory in 1885. True, Engels omits the activity of the Communist Correspondence Committees (see p. 72), to which Riazanov first drew attention. But Engels never wrote anything to suggest that he and Marx "had been sitting in their cloisters." On the contrary, he wrote that "both of us entered bag and baggage into the political movement."

Page 64

The reference to Steklov is to I. M. Steklov, *Karl Marx* (1922, in Russian).

Page 65

The League of the Just continued to exist after 1839, as shown by documents which have since come to light. It continued to function until its London congress of June 1847, when it assumed the name Communist League (see p. 74). At that time it had members in London (the headquarters), Paris, Brussels, Liége, Stockholm, and several German cities, including Hamburg and Leipzig.

Page 66

Hughes de Lamennais (1782–1854), better known as Félicité de Lamennais. Auguste Blanqui (1805–1881) was a professional revolutionary who believed in the possibility of overthrowing the capitalist system with a conspiring group of dedicated agitators.

Page 74

At this London congress Engels represented the two Paris sections of the League of the Just.

Page 75

The slogan, "Workers of all countries, unite," had already appeared in the constitution of the Communist League (*Bund der Kommunisten,* literally, League of the Communists), adopted at the June congress.

Page 76

Engels probably did not write any article for the journal (called *Kommunistische Zeitung*) which appeared in September 1847, although it shows his influence. Engels wrote two drafts for a "Communist catechism," one in June 1847, the other in October 1847. The June catechism has only recently come to light.

Page 82

Rather than "real socialism," the term commonly used is "true socialism" (*wahrer Sozialismus*), a nickname given by Marx and Engels to a kind of belletristic socialism aimed at finding the "true" man.

Page 102

Friedrich Lessner (1825–1910) was a tailor. He spent three years in prison and then emigrated to England, where he was a faithful comrade of Marx and Engels. In his later life he wrote down some of his recollections.

Page 104

Charles Dana (1819–1897) was a Harvard graduate who participated in the utopian experiment of Brook Farm near Boston (1841–1846). As a reporter he covered the revolutions of 1848 in Europe, and from 1849–

1862 was managing editor of the *New York Tribune*. After 1868 he was editor of the *New York Sun* and became a pioneer of modern news editing.

Page 118
Prince Plon-Plon was Napoléon Joseph Charles Paul Bonaparte (1822–1891), not the brother of Napoleon III, but a cousin.

Page 121
Among the documents published by the French government after the fall of Napoleon III was the receipt for 40,000 francs paid to Vogt in 1859 (mentioned in Marx's letter to Liebknecht, on or about April 10, 1871).

Page 124
This "General German Labour Union" (*Allgemeiner Deutscher Arbeiterverein*) was organized by Lassalle in May 1863. It was the beginning of the emancipation of the German working class from being an appendage of the liberal bourgeoisie. The "Open Letter" (see p. 123) was written on the eve of the founding of the GGLU.

Page 135
This "famous colloquy between the labourer and the capitalist" can be found in the chapter, "The Working Day," in section III ("The Limits of the Working Day") of *Capital*. It has an explicit reference to the London builder's strike for the reduction of the working day to nine hours. Its leader, William Randall Cremer (1838–1908), was secretary of the First International from 1864–1866, and later a liberal member of parliament.

Page 138
Georges Clémenceau (1841–1929) started, like so many French politicians, as a radical socialist. He turned to bourgeois radicalism, was known as the "tiger" for his biting irony, and, as minister of war in 1917, led France to victory against the Germans. He dominated the Versailles conference after the war.

Page 142
Edward Spencer Beesly was professor of political economy at London University. He was a democrat and, with other collaborators on *Fortnightly Review,* an admirer of Comte's positivism.

Page 163
Giuseppe Mazzini (1805–1872), an Italian bourgeois democratic revolutionary and vaguely a socialist, was one of the leaders of the Italian struggle for national liberation.

Page 182
Alexander Herzen, a Russian revolutionary democrat, lived from 1847 in France and England. He edited the influential periodical *Kolokol* (The Bell).

Page 194
The affair of Sergei Nietchayev (1847–1882) inspired Dostoevski to write *The Possessed*. Nietchayev spent the last years of his life in a tsarist prison.

Page 196

The Congress of September 1872 was held in The Hague, Netherlands (see p. 198).

Page 198

The history of the First International in the United States between 1872 and 1876 is not as colorless as it seems from Riazanov's text. By 1872 there were about thirty sections and five thousand members in the United States, spread over several cities; of the New York sections one was French, one Czech, four were German, and two native American. The International Working Man's Association (IWMA) played an important role in the unemployment struggles after the panic of 1872; its activity, however, was hampered by factional haggles. When, in 1876 at Philadelphia, delegates from nineteen sections of the IWMA met and dissolved the organization, they adopted a militant declaration with the promise to continue their struggle on a national basis, as their fellow workers in Europe were doing. A few days after the meeting of the IWMA, also at Philadelphia, many of its members assisted in forming a "Working Men's Party of the United States"; one of the founders was F. A. Sorge (see p. 215), a friend of Marx and Engels. The party changed its name to Socialist Labor Party, which still exists as a sect, but in the course of its history has harbored or inspired many leading socialists. See Philip S. Foner, *History of the Labor Movement in the United States* (New York, 1947), I, ch. 20–24, esp. pp. 450–453, and C. Reeve, *The Life and Times of Daniel DeLeon* (New York, 1972).

Page 203

Was Engels really so "hopelessly dry and cold" in his early as well as his middle years? People who knew him well have given an entirely different picture of this "merry companion, the agreeable comrade," who "always loved the company of young people, always was a hospitable host," as Paul Lafargue, whose acquaintance with Engels dated from 1867 on, wrote.

Page 204

This "certain Smith" was Adolphe Smith Headingley, a member of Hyndman's Social Democratic Federation. He was close to the "possibilists," a reformist current in the French socialist movement.

Page 205

The "postscript" mentioned in lines 14-15 is the one Marx wrote to the 1875 edition of his 1852–1853 book on the Cologne Communist trial (see p. 102). Among the important writings of this period after 1873 we must mention the *Critique of the Gotha Program*, with the *Communist Manifesto*, one of Marx's most significant programmatic works in which he deals with the transition period from capitalism to communism. Although written in 1875, it was not published until 1891, and then by Engels.

Page 209

Bernstein died in 1932.

Page 210*

The *Anti-Dühring* now exists in a full English translation (New York:

1939), as well as his "Notes" to this book which appear in *Dialectics of Nature* (New York, 1940).

Page 210†
Kautsky died in 1938.

Page 213
Vera Sassulitch died in 1919, Paul Axelrod in 1928, and Leo Deutsch in 1941.

INDEX

Selected Modern Reader Paperbacks